REMEMBERING

FLINT

MICHIGAN

I08057 87

REMEMBERING FLINT MICHIGAN

Stories from the Vehicle City

GARY FLINN

THE History PRESS

Published by The History Press
Charleston, SC 29403
www.historypress.net

Copyright © 2010 by Gary Flinn
All rights reserved

First published 2010
Updated 2024

Manufactured in the United States

ISBN 978.1.60949.018.8

Library of Congress Cataloging-in-Publication Data

Flinn, Gary.
Remembering Flint, Michigan : stories from the Vehicle City / Gary Flinn.
p. cm.
Compilation of updated articles originally published in Uncommon Sense from December 2004 to July 2007.
ISBN 978-1-60949-018-8
1. Flint (Mich.)--History. 2. Flint (Mich.)--Social life and customs. I. Uncommon sense II. Title.
F574.F62F53 2010
977.4'37--dc22
2010034442

Notice: The information in this book is true and complete to the best of our knowledge. It is offered without guarantee on the part of the author or The History Press. The author and The History Press disclaim all liability in connection with the use of this book.

All rights reserved. No part of this book may be reproduced or transmitted in any form whatsoever without prior written permission from the publisher except in the case of brief quotations embodied in critical articles and reviews.

To the readers of my articles and the staff of the Uncommon Sense *for providing ideas.*

To the memory of Charles Weinstein, who enjoyed my articles; they were found by his family in his scrapbook after his death.

Those who cannot remember the past are condemned to repeat it.

—*George Santayana,* The Life of Reason: Or the Phases of Human Progress, *1905*

Contents

Contents

Preface

This book compiles and updates articles originally published in the *Uncommon Sense* alternative newspaper from December 2004 to July 2007 and includes one piece planned for the August 2007 issue but never published because the *Uncommon Sense* folded. One article was published online only.

I have always been a history buff. History was my favorite subject in school as I received the best grades in the subject. I initially did not think of myself as a historian, but a tragic event involving a favorite historic landmark eventually got me started.

It all began in the winter of 1997, when the U.S. 23 Drive-in Theater's original screen tower burned down. When owner Lou Warrington Jr. decided to rebuild it, I decided to take pictures of the replacement screen's construction. The replacement screen tower was hoisted into position on June 30, 1997. The photos were submitted to various Internet websites devoted to drive-in theaters. One of them suggested I write an occasional column, which I did, beginning in May 2004. Staff members of the *Uncommon Sense* alternative newspaper read those pieces and asked me to write local history pieces for that publication. The pieces were written with the credo I followed: that history should be fun.

The online-only articles ended in 2007, when the webmaster and I had a falling out over a political banner ad I objected to. Those pieces are archived on my own website. In the meantime, *Your Magazine* expressed interest in my articles and began publishing them with the February 2008 issue. Because *Your Magazine* was published by the *Flint Journal*, I had access to the *Flint Journal*'s photo library, which is a treasure-trove of Flint history. With the contacts made at the *Journal*, I began doing a monthly piece in the *Flint Journal* itself on May 2008. I was doing two articles a month, one for *Your Magazine* and the other for the *Flint Journal*. While the *Your Magazine* articles were basically fluff pieces, the *Journal* editors encouraged me to continue with the style I was using for the *Uncommon Sense*.

This was made obvious when I wrote two separate articles to note the 100th anniversary of Hurley Medical Center. For the August 2008 issue of *Your Magazine*, I wrote a positive piece about the history of the hospital. The *Flint Journal* article, published on July 27, 2008, was devoted to the hospital's founder, James J. Hurley, whose will bequeathed the founding of the hospital. I noted that his and his wife's graves in Old Calvary Cemetery at the edge of a ravine were eroding. Hurley Medical Center was concerned about that angle, until cemetery management claimed sole responsibility for maintaining their graves.

Cutbacks in the newspaper business led to the folding of *Your Magazine* after June 2009, as well as the end of my regular columns in the *Flint Journal* the following month.

Despite this, many of my old *Flint Journal* articles were still found online through mlive.com and caught the interest of The History Press. Hopefully, a follow-up book can be published in association with the *Flint Journal* containing the pieces published in *Your Magazine* and the *Flint Journal*.

This is the first book I have written with stories from the Vehicle City. History is a continuing process, and because of that, there have been a few changes regarding people, places and institutions since *Remembering Flint Michigan: Stories from the Vehicle City* was first published in 2010. These updates appear at the end of certain chapters throughout this reprinted edition, as well as in the preface of my second book, *Hidden History of Flint* (2017).

Acknowledgements

My thanks go to *Uncommon Sense* publisher Matt Zacks for granting permission to reuse the articles for this book, as well as my editor at The History Press, Joseph Gartrell. Additional thanks go to the staff of the Sloan Museum and the Flint Public Library, where much of my research took place. Much of the research at the Flint Public Library included use of the microfilm files of newspapers and the many volumes of Flint city directories dating back to the nineteenth century, most of which were published by R.L. Polk and Company. Special thanks go to the Flint Public Library's resident historian, Michael Madden, as well as Randy Farb and Myra Gullett. At the Sloan Museum, the Buick Gallery and Research Center exhibits were especially useful. Special thanks go to museum staff members Jane McIntosh, Jeff Taylor and Sara Flore. Thanks also to those who provided encouragement and materials for this book, including Shawn Chittle, Tom Wirt and Matt Collins.

A Trip to Flint's Historic Cemeteries

We start remembering Flint, Michigan, by paying visits to three of Flint's oldest surviving cemeteries, one of which has the stones, if not the bones, of Flint's earliest cemetery. Among the graves are those of Flint's pioneers and developers.

The oldest surviving cemetery in the immediate Flint area is Old Calvary Cemetery, a Catholic cemetery located on North Ballenger Highway (formerly Frontenac Boulevard) between Flushing Road and the Flint River, just outside the city in Flint Township. It was founded as Calvary Catholic Cemetery in 1847, while Flint was still a village, and got its present name after New Calvary Cemetery was developed in 1928. This cemetery was developed along the Flint River, and the original entrance was on Flushing Road, where a since-abandoned road connected the cemetery with Flushing Road. The entrance was moved after a parcel of land that fronts Ballenger Highway was acquired to expand the cemetery. This cemetery has a circle reserved for the burial of highly regarded priests. The most recognizable priest buried there is Father Norman DuKette (1890–1980), the founder of Christ the King Catholic Church on Lapeer Road.

As with many old cemeteries, you can tell the socioeconomic status of the families buried in the cemetery by the markers used. The more prosperous departed were buried with granite markers, which last practically forever. I found one marker, made of "white bronze," that the Stanton family

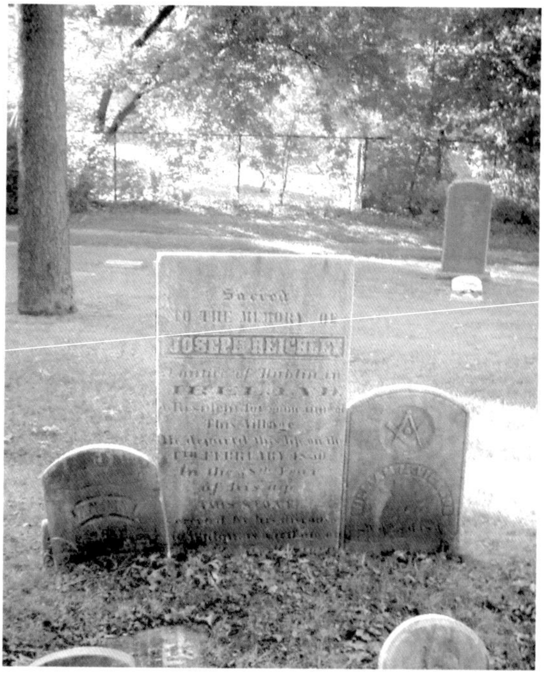

Pioneer's Row at Avondale Cemetery, including Joseph Reighley's marker.

commissioned from the American White Bronze Company of Chicago in 1887. It was fabricated using zinc, which is resistant to corrosion, and is in remarkably good condition. It has outlasted its concrete base, which is crumbling. The many others who were less prosperous had less expensive soft marble stones, which unfortunately have lost their lettering to the weather over the decades. Among the notable people buried at Old Calvary are Peter Lennon (died 1891 at age fifty-two), a prosperous farmer after whom Lennon Road and the village of Lennon were named; Daniel O'Sullivan (died 1872 at age seventy-two), Flint's first schoolteacher; Frank J. Manley (1903–1972), who pioneered the community school movement here in Flint; James J. Hurley (1849–1905), whose will bequeathed the founding of what is now Hurley Medical Center; and William Hamilton (1827–1904), mayor of Flint, local lumber baron and the man on whose farm the Buick City complex was developed. The Hamilton plot also has the most impressive marker at Old Calvary Cemetery, a large granite cross with the Hamilton name on its base. Of course, Hamilton Avenue was named in his honor. In 1876, a Catholic family could buy a lot at Old Calvary that included six graves for ten dollars. The interment fee that year was two dollars.

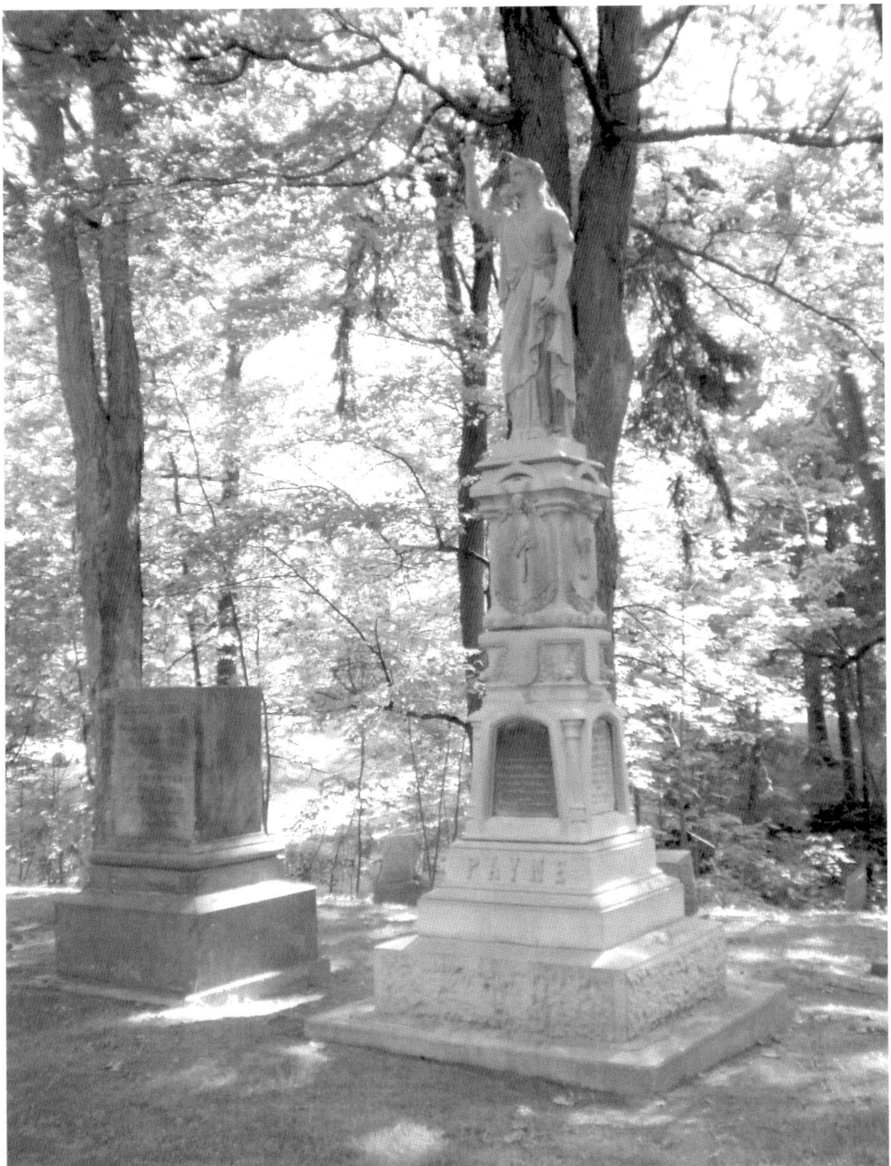

Chauncey Payne's white bronze marker at Glenwood Cemetery towers over his father-in-law Jacob Smith's marker.

The second-oldest surviving cemetery in the area and the oldest in the city of Flint is Glenwood Cemetery, at 2500 West Court Street, which can proudly proclaim itself "Flint's Historic Cemetery." A Michigan historic marker is at the entrance and provides the history behind this cemetery. A virtual who's who in Flint history can be found at Glenwood. Flint's first white settler, Jacob Smith (1780–1825, though the stone erroneously reads 1773–1825) is buried here. So are several former Flint mayors, including Charles Stewart Mott (1875–1973). Michigan governor and local sawmill owner Henry Crapo (1804–1869) is buried here. So are another governor, Josiah Begole (1815–1896), and a few congressmen, including George Durand (1838–1903), after whom the city of Durand was named. Carriage makers J. Dallas Dort (1861–1925) and James Whiting (1842–1919) are buried here. So is General Motors president Harlow Curtice (1893–1962). Grocery chain cofounder Kamol Hamady (1893–1969) is buried here, as is banker and Bishop Airport founder Arthur G. Bishop (1851–1944). There are many other notable people buried at Glenwood, but space limitations prevent their inclusion here.

Glenwood Cemetery is also noted for its rolling hills and marvelous mixture of various styles of markers. Glenwood is a peaceful place to be in the middle of the city. Early Flint developer Chauncey Payne's (1795–1877) large white bronze marker, made by the Detroit Bronze Co. in Detroit, is among the most impressive in the cemetery, in contrast to his father-in-law and Flint founder Jacob Smith's rather plain tombstone next to it. Another interesting marker is the shamrock-shaped one for fish merchant John M. Donlan (1913–1987) that clearly showed his Irish heritage. This marker also shows a cross to express his faith and a fish to express his occupation.

Across town, Avondale Cemetery at 833 Chavez Drive (formerly Lewis Street, formerly Richfield Road) was founded in 1878. Unlike Glenwood, there are very few notable persons buried here. Two of them were Flint mayors; they are Clark B. Dibble (1860–1932), mayor in 1901–02, and John R. MacDonald (1857–1946), mayor in 1914–15. I've included this cemetery because it has a special section at the rear called Pioneer's Row, which features approximately 122 ancient and not-so-ancient markers placed together. These stones were moved from the nearby Old City Cemetery on Lewis Street, where eastbound Longway Boulevard, a Social Security office and the Holiday Inn Express are located today. The city redeveloped the cemetery site and put the land back on the public tax rolls when Longway

Boulevard was built in 1958. The last burial at Old City Cemetery took place in 1940. Beginning in 1952, the city moved 1,199 bodies, including 925 unidentified, to the newer City Cemetery at Linden Road, near Pasadena Avenue. Some bodies were buried in buckskins, and others were buried on top of one another. Other remains were reburied by family members in other cemeteries. There were approximately 1,800 burials in the Old City Cemetery, established in 1836. When the Holiday Inn Express was being built as the Hampton Inn in the mid-1980s, several human bones from the old cemetery were found. They were reburied at the current City Cemetery.

I visited the current City Cemetery on Linden Road and Pasadena Avenue in 2005 and was shocked at its condition. The markers were few and far between. If it hadn't been for the wooden crosses marking where veterans were buried, I wouldn't have known that any were buried there. Behind the trees along Linden Road, most parts of the cemetery looked as if they hadn't been mowed all year. Most of the markers for the veterans were provided free by the United States. The oldest marker I could read was flat on the ground, and it indicated that the person died in 1892. The City Cemetery seemed to have developed into a paupers' graveyard. Upon returning to City Cemetery in 2009, it was neatly mowed and better maintained.

Among the stones at Avondale Cemetery's Pioneer's Row are at least three that predate the city. My favorite reads:

> *Sacred to the Memory of Joseph Reighley, a native of Dublin in Ireland. A resident of some time of this village. He departed this life on the 4th February 1850 in the 38th year of his age. This stone is erected by his "disconso late"* [sic] *widow as a tribute of respect to his memory.*

I wonder if the ghost of Mr. Reighley is somewhere between Avondale and City Cemeteries, as his remains were separated from his marker. With all the stones bunched together at the back of Avondale in Pioneer's Row, this could be the setting for a spooky Halloween story.

Stockton Center at Spring Grove

In 1872, one of Flint's leading families built their new home on Ann Arbor Street at what was then the west end of town. It was described by the local newspaper of that time, the *Wolverine Citizen*, as elegant and "among the most stylish and spacious of the many handsome first-class houses in our city." The two-story, Italianate-style house was built on a four-and-a-half-acre treed hillside site described as "pleasure grounds." The mineral spring on the site inspired the Stocktons to name their home Spring Grove.

Four generations of the Stockton family would live in that house. The patriarch who built the house was Colonel Thomas Baylis Whitmarsh Stockton (1805–1890). An 1827 graduate of the U.S. Military Academy at West Point, he spent much of his military career as a topographical engineer in the Midwest. In 1834, he laid out the turnpike that linked Detroit and Saginaw, along which Flint developed where the road crossed the Flint River. As a colonel, he raised the First Michigan Infantry Regiment to fight in the Mexican War and Stockton's Independent Regiment (the Sixteenth Michigan) to fight in the Civil War. Captured at Gaines Mill, Virginia, in June 1862, he was held at Libby Prison for two months. Stockton left the army in 1862 and settled permanently in Flint.

The matriarch was Maria Smith Stockton (1813–1898), a daughter of Flint founder Jacob Smith. Under her Chippewa name, *Nondashemau*, she,

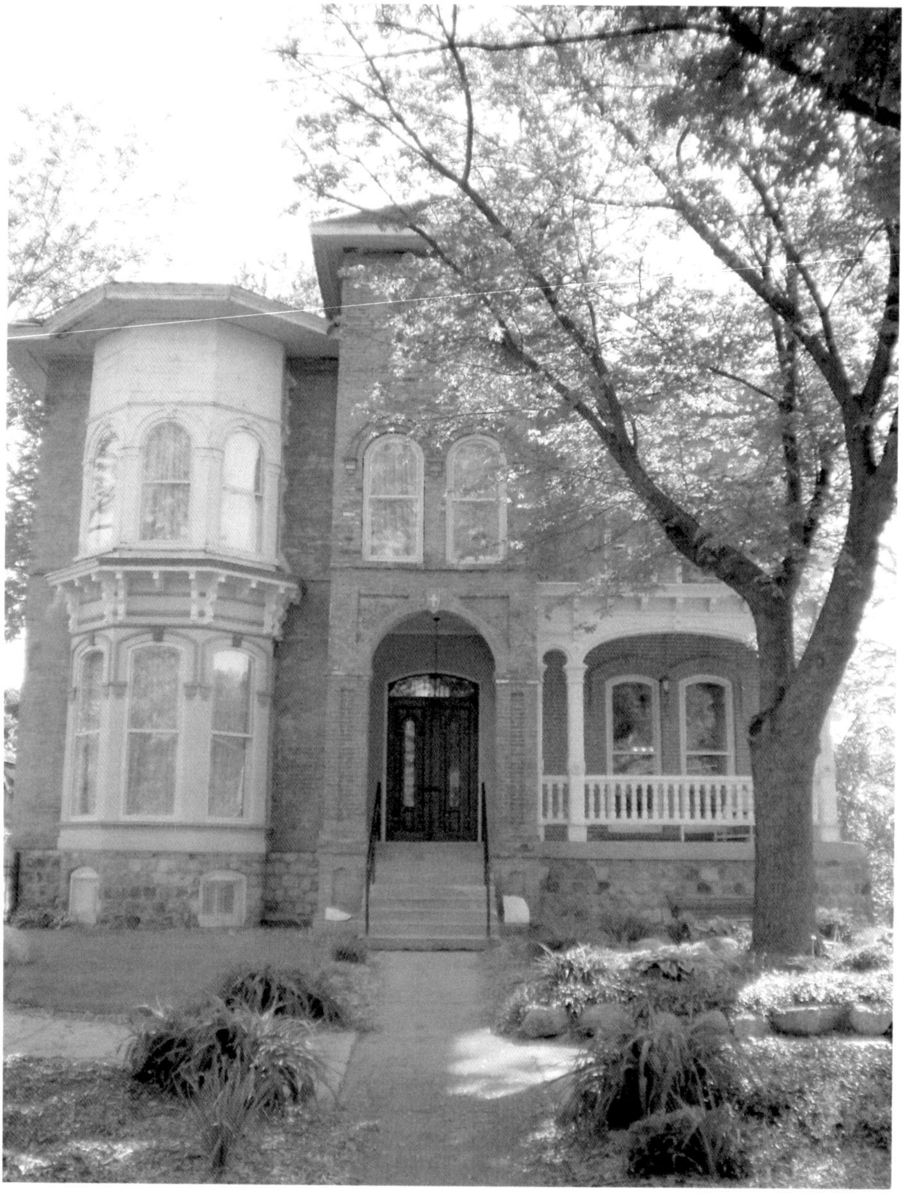

Stockton Center today.

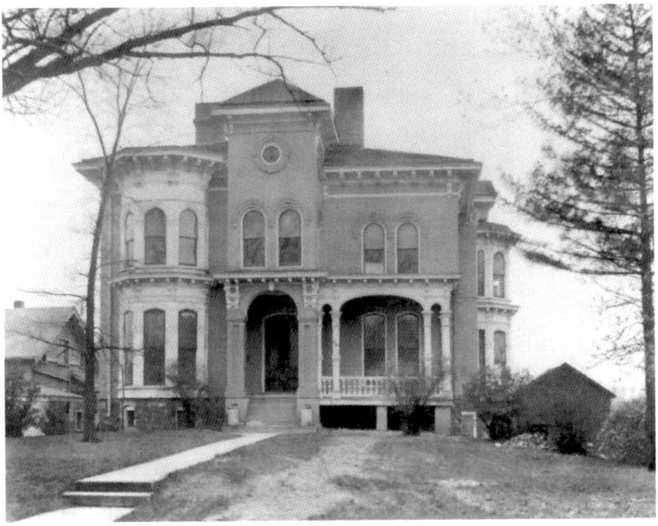

Stockton House when it was the Stockton family home. *Courtesy of Freeman Greer.*

along with her siblings, was awarded a large tract of land in present-day Flint under the Saginaw Treaty of 1819 between the United States and the Chippewa Nation. In 1851, she led the formation of the city's Ladies Library Association, the forerunner of the Flint Public Library.

Their son, Baylis Stockton (1832–1918), continued to live in the house with his wife, Maria McGreavey Stockton (1836–1919). Their son, Thomas F. Stockton (1870–1937), who became a prominent attorney, continued to live in the house with his first wife, Alma (1876–1913). After Alma's death, Thomas married his second wife, Elizabeth (1872–1951).

Around 1915, the address of the house was changed from 716 Ann Arbor Street to 720 Ann Arbor Street.

The deaths of both his father in 1918 and his mother in 1919 seemed to affect Tom and his family greatly, and they moved out of the large house in 1919 and into the Blackstone Apartments at 313 East Second Street on the other side of downtown. This apartment building was torn down about 1967 to make way for a parking lot.

The house was sold in 1921 to the Sisters of St. Joseph. They established the first St. Joseph Hospital in that house, the forerunner of today's Genesys Health Systems. A notable reminder of St. Joseph Hospital's years of occupancy at Stockton House is a keystone with a cross over the front entrance. The rear of the building was added on to several times to accommodate the city's growing medical needs. But by the mid-1930s, the site had proved too small, and the Sisters of St. Joseph built a new St. Joseph Hospital where Mott Community College's Regional Technology Center is now located. They moved out of the house in 1936.

In 1937, the house became the Union Rescue Mission, led by superintendent Carl Rhoades. This rescue mission has no direct connection with the present Carriage Town Ministries, which was founded as the Rescue Mission of Flint in 1950.

By 1945, Stockton House began a long life as either a nursing home or a home for the aged. Hynd's Convalescent Hospital and Home was run by supervisor Mrs. Elizabeth Hynd. A decade later, it became the Kith Haven Nursing Home. After Kith Haven moved to its present location at G-1059 North Ballenger Highway on May 22, 1970, the house became the Cecilia Home for the Aged. In 1984, it was renamed to Stockton House.

Stockton House as a home for the aged closed in 1996, but three occupants of the home were still living there in 1997. By 1998, the occupants were down to one, and then the home was vacant from 1999 onward.

In 2002, For Flint Investments, a partnership of Freeman Greer, Renee Greer and James McCluskey, purchased the house. It is being renovated, with much of the house being restored to its original appearance, including the front façade. The restoration of the facility is following the secretary of the interior's guidelines for restoration. The restoration process has proved to be quite a challenge. The plaster walls and wood floor had been damaged by water from a leaking roof. The roofs have been repaired, and the damaged plaster and wood floors have all been repaired. All the wood floors had been covered with asphalt paper and linoleum, making them difficult to uncover for restoration, but this did help to protect the original floors from the water. The floors consist of oak, maple and cherry hardwoods. An analysis of the original paint colors has also been completed as part of the restoration.

The original design of the house used stars on the walls and throughout the building as a reminder of the colonel's military history. A few pictures from the St. Joseph Hospital era have offered a glimpse of some of the missing parts of the original building, such as the fireplace mantel. Other pictures show the chapel that existed in the main tower and the operating room in the hospital addition. The renovators of the facility are relying on these pictures and site investigation to restore the facility to its former glory for future generations to enjoy.

Stockton House is listed in the National Register of Historic Places. A Michigan Historical Marker was dedicated on June 18, 2005.

Now called the Stockton Center at Spring Grove, the home serves as a professional office building with a public museum. The building has eleven thousand square feet of leasable space.

The Stockton House is an important part of Flint's heritage and a visible link to Flint history, with connections to Flint's origins and the histories of Genesys Health Systems and present-day Kith Haven.

Thanks to Stockton Center at Spring Grove owner and architect Freeman Greer, as well as the staff of Kith Haven Nursing Home. The chronology was based on information found in city directory listings for the Stockton House address.

David Buick

A Forgotten Auto Pioneer

Buick. It's a name associated with cars, the brand that launched General Motors Corporation and the reason Flint developed into a major automotive center. But the man behind the name, David Buick, became a footnote in automotive history, forgotten even in his native Scotland.

David Dunbar Buick was born in Arbroath, Scotland, on September 17, 1854, but immigrated with his family to the United States when he was two, settling in Detroit. His father died when he was five. His mother then worked at a candy store to support the family. At age fifteen, David Buick went to work for the Alexander Manufacturing Company, which made plumbing fixtures. When that company folded, there were no takers for the physical facilities, so Buick persuaded William Sherwood, an old schoolmate, to buy the company with him, and the Buick & Sherwood Manufacturing Company was formed in 1882.

The company became successful in part because Buick developed a method to adhere porcelain to wrought iron to make bathtubs. Buick made improvements to other plumbing fixtures and improved on the lawn sprinkler. But Buick was not content with being a successful plumbing-fixture maker. He developed an obsession for gasoline engines and the horseless carriage that did not please Sherwood, who had the business skills Buick didn't have. Sherwood wanted Buick to stick with plumbing. Buick sold his interest in Buick & Sherwood for $100,000 in 1899 and used the proceeds to form the

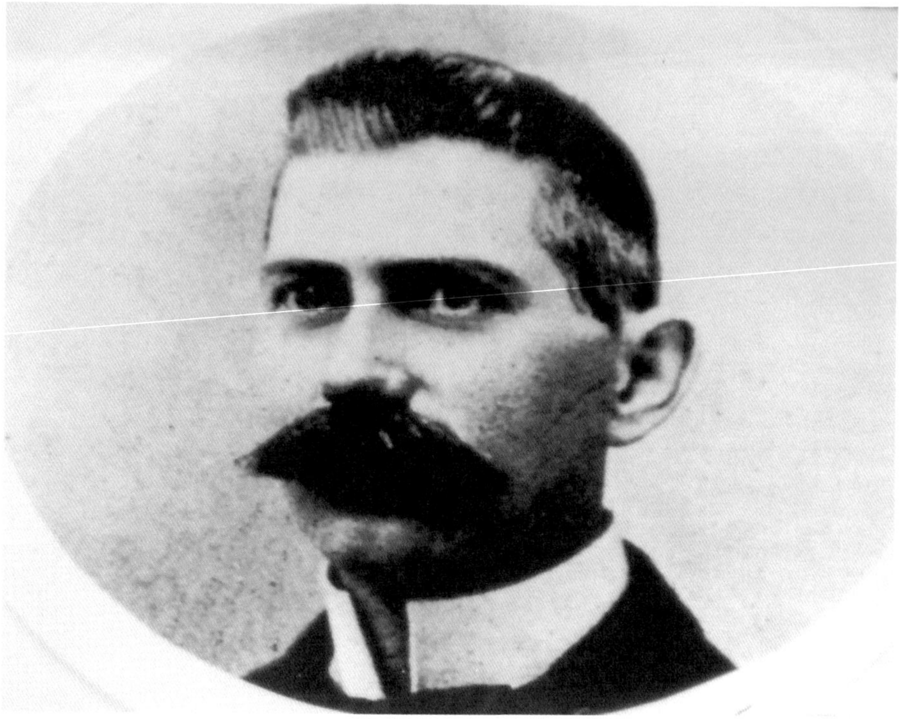

David Buick.

Buick Auto Vim and Power Company, which produced stationary gasoline engines for farm use.

By 1901, Buick had built his first automobile with the help of an associate, machinist Walter Marr. Buick made a formal offer to Marr on April 5 to sell the car for $300. Marr bought it for $225 on August 26. In 1902, the Buick Manufacturing Company was formed, and Buick developed the "valve-in-head" gasoline engine, which became the standard of the industry. Buick was a great inventor, but he had a temperamental demeanor and couldn't keep his head above water financially. He borrowed $5,000 from another friend and sheet metal supplier Benjamin Briscoe Jr., whom Buick already owed money, and formed Buick Motor Company in 1903. The firm's capitalization was $100,000 in stock, with Briscoe holding $99,700 worth of stock and Buick just $300 worth. But Briscoe decided to invest in another car company, the Maxwell-Briscoe Motor Company, with Jonathan Maxwell (a company that evolved into Chrysler), and a deal was made with the Flint

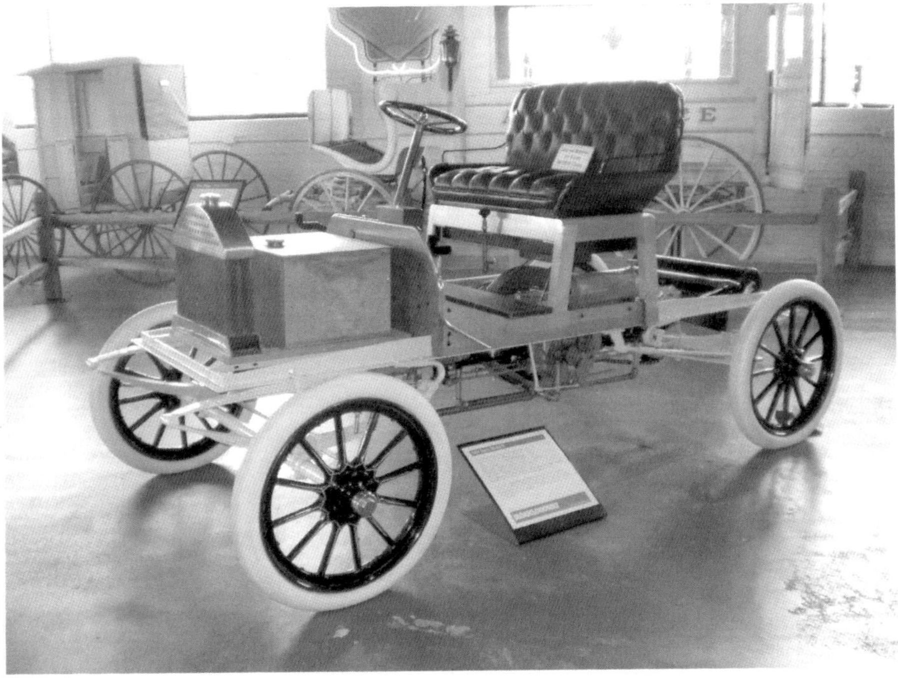

Replica of a 1904 Buick Model B, as it looked on its July 9, 1904 test run, at the Buick Gallery.

Wagon Works, led by James H. Whiting, to buy the Buick Motor Company. As part of the deal, the company would move from Detroit to Flint. Buick was president, and Whiting was general manager. David Buick's move to Flint was held up until arrangements were made to cover his $11,000 in debts. The company built thirty-seven Model B Buicks in 1904. One of the cars was given to William C. Durant, who ran the Durant-Dort Carriage Company, the largest maker of horse-drawn carriages in the United States. The Buick Motor Company developed financial problems again, but Durant, an excellent salesman, believed in the car and took over the company. Durant and his backers increased the Buick Motor Company's capitalization to $500,000 and secured subscriptions to $250,000 of the stock.

While Buick was still president, Durant was effectively running the company. Buick and Durant clashed over the direction of the company. Durant believed in mass production, while Buick had a one-car-at-a-time production mentality. In 1906, fifty-two-year-old Buick left the company he founded and returned to Detroit. Two years later, he made the mistake of his life by selling his Buick stock to Durant for $100,000. Durant formed a holding company in 1908, General Motors (GM), with Buick as a division of GM. Former partner Briscoe estimated in 1921 that if Buick had held onto his Buick stock, it would have been worth $10 million.

Buick tried other things such as oil and mining, unsuccessfully. Bad investments wiped out his settlement from Durant. Other automotive ventures produced nothing. Toward the end of his life, he was reduced to low-paying jobs. In 1928, he was an inspector at the Detroit School of Trades. He couldn't afford a telephone, let alone a new Buick. He was interviewed that year by a young newspaper reporter, later a famous Civil War author, Bruce Catton. Buick expressed no regrets over what had happened and was not bitter toward Billy Durant. By that time, Durant had been forced out of General Motors twice, and his own company, Durant Motors, would go bankrupt in 1933. But that's another story.

Durant himself said of Buick:

> *David Buick was a likeable fellow. But he was a dreamer, and he couldn't be practical. He tried most every kind of business. Yet he never seemed to settle down. We did everything we could at the plant to make it easy for him. We arranged for his son, Tom, to be on the payroll and to keep his father settled. But after some years he just drifted away.*

David Buick died on March 5, 1929, of colon cancer at age seventy-four in Harper Hospital in Detroit. He was buried at Woodmere Cemetery in Detroit. Buick's death was reported on the front page of the following day's issue of the *Flint Daily Journal*, which printed two articles about David Buick and the company he founded. Had Buick been a better businessman, he would have been a wealthy man. But he was an inventor, not an organizer of automotive production. His birthplace at 26 Green Street in Arbroath, Scotland, was torn down several years ago to make way for a housing development. General Motors placed a plaque where Green Street once was to note the location of Buick's birthplace. That brass plaque corroded in the salty air of this harbor town and was replaced by a bronze plaque. The original plaque was cleaned up and relocated to the Buick Gallery and Research Center, at the corner of Walnut Street and Longway Boulevard near the Cultural Center, where it is on display.

DRIVING UNDERNEATH THE ARCHES

On November 29, 2003, a part of downtown Flint's past officially returned to become part of Flint's present and future when the replicated Flint Vehicle City arches were dedicated and lit for the first time. The arches are reminders of Flint's glorious past as the "Vehicle City" as it faces an uncertain future.

The vehicles that were made in Flint when the original arches were built were horse-drawn carriages. The leading maker of horse-drawn carriages in Flint was the Durant-Dort Carriage Company, co-founded by William C. Durant and J. Dallas Dort and in business from 1886 to 1917. Both men would also start companies that made horseless carriages. Dort founded the Dort Motor Car Company, which was in business from 1915 to 1923. Dort Highway was named in his honor. Durant took over the then-small Buick Motor Company in 1904 and made it the leading motorcar company by 1908, the year Durant founded Buick's parent company, General Motors Corporation.

The first arches were erected in 1899 and built by Genesee Iron Works. The arches were each fitted with fifty light bulbs that were illuminated at night; they replaced gas lighting. To celebrate Flint's Golden Jubilee in 1905, an additional arch was erected near the point where Saginaw Street and Detroit Street (now M.L. King Avenue) split off north of the bridge over the Flint River. This arch was topped off by an illuminated sign reading,

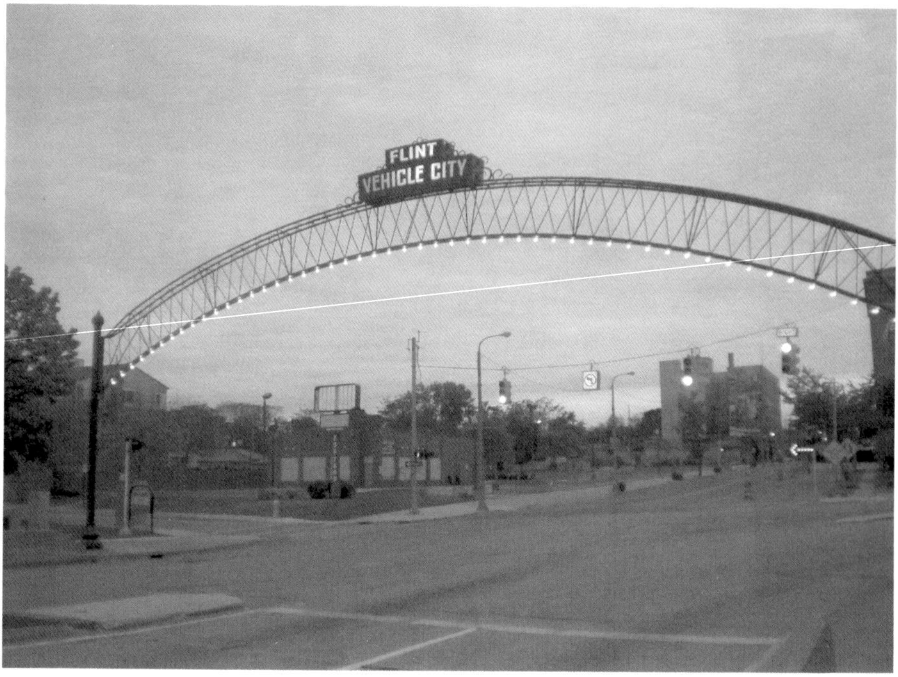

The Vehicle City arch lit at sunset.

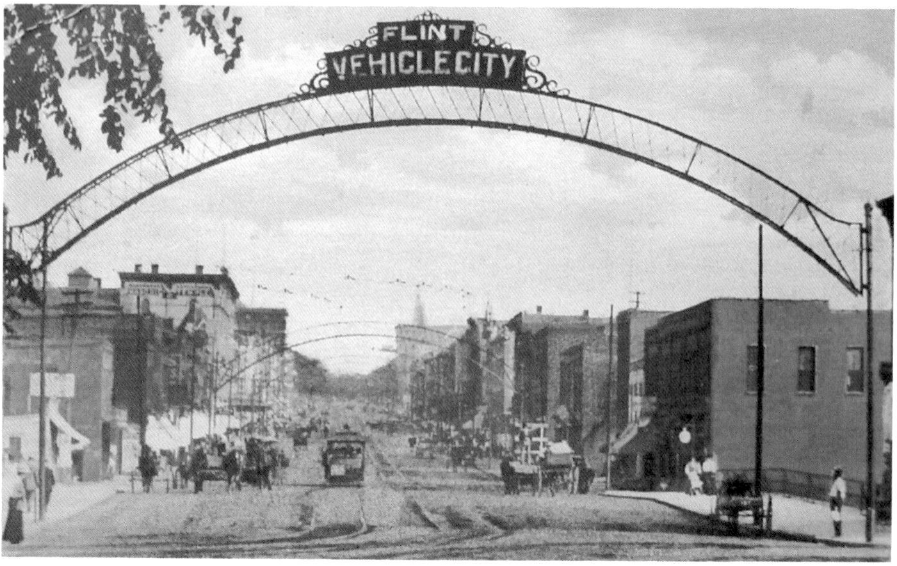

A vintage postcard of the original Vehicle City arch.

"Flint, Vehicle City." For the Christmas holiday season, the regular light bulbs were replaced by multicolored light bulbs. That tradition was resumed in recent years with the new arches during the holiday season from Thanksgiving to New Year's Day.

There are seven arches over Saginaw Street from Court Street to north of the Flint River Bridge, where the "Vehicle City" arch stands. The pictures included in this chapter show how the original arches looked then and how the replicated arches look now.

In 1919, the Flint City Council ordered the arches taken down and replaced by boulevard lighting. A plan to move the arches to Flint's major entry points never materialized, so the arches were scrapped.

The new arches are part of a series of downtown Flint beautification projects and were paid for by private funds. Other beautification projects include new sidewalks and the rebuilding of Saginaw Street between Court Street and the Flint River with the paving bricks retained.

In May 2008, two additional arches were added south of Court Street, one in front of the Genesee County Court House and the other—topped off by a sign reading, "Flint, Genesee County," to greet drivers arriving downtown from I-69—between city hall and the Genesee County administration building. Smaller arch designs enhance the I-69 service drive to downtown.

BANKS FROM FLINT'S PAST

In 2006, Citizens Bank and Ann Arbor–based Republic Bank merged to form Citizens Republic Bancorp, still operating as Citizens Bank. That was the last example of the merging of banks and savings and loan associations in Flint. Other banks were swallowed up by larger out-of-town banks. Two failed during the Great Depression in 1933. This chapter recalls banks from Flint's past.

While Citizens Bank has the oldest roots in Flint, it began in 1871 under a slightly different name: Citizens National Bank. It gave up its national bank charter and became Citizens Commercial & Savings Bank, or Citizens Bank, in 1890 under a State of Michigan charter. The oldest city directory on the Flint Public Library shelves from 1872 lists Citizens National Bank and First National Bank. First National Bank had even older roots, going back to the first successful bank in Flint, the Exchange Bank, formed in 1858. In 1865, the Exchange Bank was rechartered as First National Bank. It became Flint National Bank in 1885 and the National Bank of Flint in 1905.

In 1872, the Genesee County Savings Bank, or Genesee Bank, was founded. It acquired the National Bank of Flint in 1916. This left Flint without a nationally chartered bank, so all of the Flint banks were chartered by the State of Michigan. Genesee Bank spun off the acquired bank in 1918 and received a new national bank charter, becoming First National Bank again. Its slogan was: "The only bank in the county under federal control."

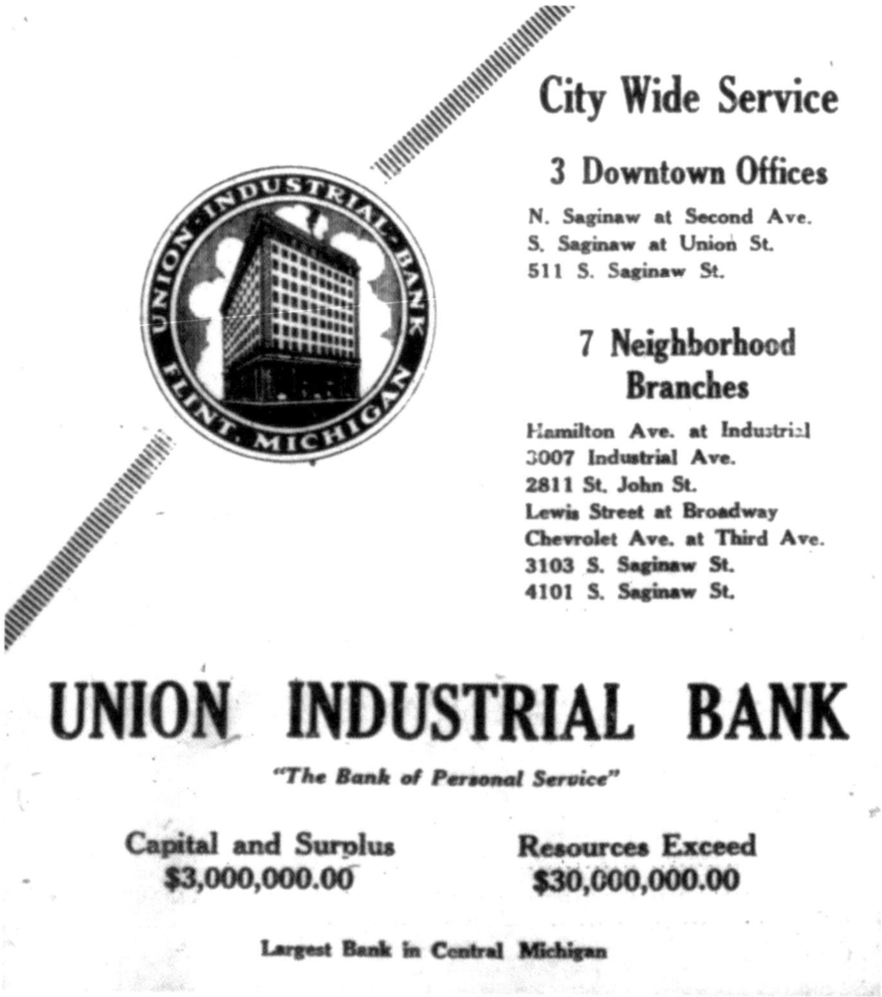

A print ad for Union Industrial Bank.

Nationally chartered banks, by law, must have the word "National" in their names or the initials "N.A.," for National Association, following them.

In 1893, the Union Trust & Savings Bank opened. In 1909, Industrial Savings Bank was formed. Industrial Savings Bank was unique in that its first office was not downtown but across from the Buick factory at the northwest corner of Hamilton and Industrial Avenues. When the Flint P. Smith Building, later the Sill Building, opened in 1911, Industrial Savings Bank established its main office there. In 1922, Industrial Savings Bank moved its

STATEMENT OF CONDITION
June 30, 1938

RESOURCES

Cash and Due from Banks	$1,004,285.26	
U. S. Government Securities	2,127,215.35	$3,131,500.61
Other Bonds and Securities		1,445,200.73
Federal Reserve Bank Stock		20,100.00
Loans and Discounts		384,607.67
Real Estate Mortgages		462,378.58
Furniture and Fixtures		1.00
Income Accrued Receivable, Net		17,268.87
Total Resources		$5,461,057.46

LIABILITIES

Deposits		$4,541,051.50
Capital Account:		
Common Stock	$ 400,000.00	
Surplus	275,000.00	
Undivided Profits	127,308.80	802,308.80
Reserves:		
Common Stock Dividend	5,000.00	
Contingencies	69,100.00	
Interest, Taxes, Expenses, Etc.	43,597.16	117,697.16
Total Liabilities		$5,461,057.46

NATIONAL BANK
OF FLINT

Established January 30, 1934 Complete Trust Facilities

MEMBER FEDERAL DEPOSIT INSURANCE CORPORATION

A 1938 National Bank of Flint ad.

main office to its new high-rise at North Saginaw Street and Second Avenue. Today, it's the Northbank Center, and you can still see Industrial Savings Bank inscribed on its front façade. The Union Trust & Savings Bank and the Industrial Savings Bank consolidated in 1929 as Union Industrial Bank. The following year, in 1930, Union Industrial Bank's new headquarters, the tallest building in Flint, opened on the site of the old Union Trust & Savings Bank location. The chairman of the board of Union Industrial Bank was Charles Stewart Mott.

In 1927, the Merchants & Mechanics Bank, or M&M Bank, was formed. Its main office at 120 West First Street downtown is now the Universal Building.

Savings and loan associations were first called building and loan associations. The first one to open was the short-lived Flint Savings Association in 1915. The following year, the Detroit & Northern Michigan Building & Loan Association opened its Flint office. Later called Detroit & Northern Savings & Loan Association, or D&N, it was headquartered in the upper-peninsula city of Hancock. Two other short-lived savings and loans were the Modern Building & Savings Association and the Co-operative Savings & Loan Association, both founded in 1922.

With the prosperity that Flint and the nation enjoyed in the 1920s, there were temptations. In 1928, unbeknownst to Mott, fifteen officers and tellers of the Union Industrial Bank began a scheme to invest depositors' money in the booming stock market. Even the bank president's son was in on the scheme. On October 29, 1929, the stock market crashed, causing losses of $50 billion and sparking the Great Depression. That day, the investments the "league of gentlemen" had made led to losses estimated by Frank Montague, a bank vice-president who led the scheme, at $3,592,000. The following day, Mott demanded that each of the conspirators resign and sent them home. After contacting the public prosecutor, Mott withdrew the exact amount of the losses from his own private bank account in Detroit and led a convoy of three armored cars, delivering the cash to the Union Industrial Bank to reimburse the losses. The conspirators received sentences ranging from six months to ten years for embezzlement.

The Great Depression claimed two Flint banks. The Union Industrial Bank was one, and the First National Bank was the other. They closed, along with every bank in the United States, during the 1933 Bank Holiday and never reopened. The impounded deposits of the two closed banks were freed by the formation of a new bank, the National Bank of Flint, which proudly displayed on its logo that it was established on January 30, 1934. It opened at 9:00 a.m. the following day and was located at the former Union Industrial Bank headquarters in what is now the Mott Foundation Building. On October 25, 1934, the First Federal Savings & Loan Association of Flint was formed.

In 1942, Lansing-based Michigan National Bank bought the National Bank of Flint, making Flint the seventh city served by Michigan National. Most of the other banks and savings and loans only served the Flint area, though Detroit & Northern also served Detroit and Hancock. Michigan National Bank was stymied by state banking laws and could only set up branch offices in its home city of Lansing. So until the early 1970s, Michigan National Bank in Flint could only be located downtown. Michigan National Bank got around the restriction when it opened its downtown drive-thru location in 1962 (now a Chase drive-thru), at 212 West First Street at Beach, by connecting it with the main office in the Mott Foundation Building via a pneumatic tube. When Michigan lawmakers allowed for the establishment of bank holding companies, Michigan National Corporation was formed. In 1973, it established Michigan National Bank–Mid-Michigan as a separate bank based in Flint that could establish branch offices. It eventually took over the Michigan National Bank office downtown.

In 1957, Genesee County Savings Bank and Merchants & Mechanics Bank merged to create Genesee Merchants Bank & Trust Company. All four M&M Bank locations became Genesee Merchants Bank locations. Of its three branch offices, its Dort Highway location is now Southfield Gold & Diamonds. The Franklin Avenue location closed many years ago as the neighborhood deteriorated. The Fenton Road location is now a Rite Aid pharmacy, but successor bank Chase still has its drive-thru branch behind Rite Aid on Atherton Road. At the old Genesee Bank Building at 352 South Saginaw Street, you can still see "Genesee County Savings Bank" inscribed on the façade facing Kearsley Street and a faded "Genesee County Savings Bank" painted sign on its north wall.

In 1982, First Federal Savings & Loan of Flint was purchased by Detroit & Northern Savings & Loan, and First Federal of Flint locations became D&N locations. The S&L was converted into a Federal Savings Bank in 1990 and became D&N Bank. In 1999, D&N was acquired by Republic Bank, which was founded in Flint in 1985.

In 1984, the holding company of Genesee Merchants Bank (which shortened its marketing name to Genesee Bank in the 1960s) was purchased by NBD Bancorp and became NBD Genesee Bank. When banking laws were loosened in 1988, allowing for banks to operate branches statewide, NBD Genesee Bank parent, NBD Bancorp, changed the name of its flagship bank from National Bank of Detroit to NBD Bank, N.A., and the Genesee name disappeared. The huge "Genesee Bank" neon sign atop Genesee Towers was dismantled and hauled away by helicopter. Michigan National Corporation was able to consolidate all of its subsidiary banks and operated as Michigan National Bank.

By the mid-1990s, state banking laws had loosened further, allowing out-of-state banks to operate in Michigan. In 1995, NBD Bancorp merged with First Chicago Corp. to create First Chicago NBD Corp., with the banks maintaining their identities. That changed in 1998, when First Chicago NBD merged with Columbus, Ohio–based Banc One. The merged company was based in Chicago and adopted the Bank One name for itself and its banks. New York–based J.P. Morgan Chase bought Bank One in 2004 and phased in the renaming of Bank One branches to Chase branches, finally reaching Flint in the spring of 2006.

Michigan National Corporation struggled to remain independent but was finally acquired by the National Bank of Australia in 1995. The Dutch financial company ABN AMRO acquired Michigan National Corporation in 2001 and, later that year, merged it with its own Standard Federal Bank, a Federal Savings Bank based in the Detroit area, adopting Michigan National Bank's national bank charter so the bank became Standard Federal Bank, N.A. In 2005, Standard Federal Bank, N.A., changed its name to LaSalle Bank Midwest, N.A., in a brand consolidation with ABN AMRO's flagship bank in the United States: Chicago-based LaSalle Bank, N.A. LaSalle was sold in 2007 to Bank of America, and the signs were changed again the following year.

While this article limits itself to banks that operated in the city of Flint, one bank operating in Flint's suburbs and in the city on Ballenger Highway deserves mention because of its unusual-sounding name. The Owosso Savings Bank (founded in 1886) changed its name to Pacesetter Bank & Trust in 1979 as it expanded far outside its Owosso base. It was purchased in 1984 by Grand Rapids–based Old Kent Bank, which in turn was acquired by Cincinnati, Ohio–based Fifth Third Bank in 2001. Fifth Third Bank was created by the merger of the Fifth National Bank and the Third National Bank to form the Fifth Third National Bank in Cincinnati in 1908. It chose that name instead of Third Fifth because of that term's connection with distilled spirits.

Chronology found in city directory listings, with material found in the book The Day the Bubble Burst: A Social History of the Wall Street Crash of 1929 *by Gordon Thomas and Max Morgan-Witts (1979).*

Update: In 2013, Citizens Republic Bancorp, parent company of Citizens Bank, was sold and absorbed into Akron, Ohio–based FirstMerit Bank. FirstMerit was, in turn, sold in August 2016 to Columbus, Ohio–based Huntington Bancshares, parent company of the Huntington National Bank, which entered the Flint area marketplace when it bought the local operations of Bank of America in 2014.

When Mass Transit Used Electricity

In 1956, Flint's mass transit system retired the last of its electrically powered trolley buses. With the high price of diesel fuel, the Mass Transportation Authority, the current operator of Flint's mass transit system, probably wishes it still had trolley buses.

Flint's transit system began in 1903, when the Detroit United Railway (DUR), which ran an interurban line to Detroit in 1901, began local transit service using streetcars. The streetcars ran on light railway tracks on Flint city streets and were powered by six hundred volts DC from overhead lines. A long pole sent the power from the overhead trolley line to the streetcar's electric motor. Bonded rail joints on the tracks provided the ground return to complete the circuit. Because the streetcars ran on electricity, there were no exhaust fumes.

Local transit service initially began when the interurban line was extended to serve the Buick factory. Another interurban line, the Saginaw & Flint Railway unit of Michigan Railway, began service from Saginaw to Flint in 1908. The two interurban lines overlapped on North Saginaw Street for one block, between Witherbee Street and Hamilton Avenue, leading to a nasty and often violent jurisdictional dispute. There were high stakes in the dispute over whether the DUR or Michigan Railway would develop the Flint transit system. DUR won out but did give Michigan Railway trackage rights for its interurban line and made concessions to help develop the

TROLLEY COACH SERVICE BEGINS ON DEC. 6th

OVER NORTH SAGINAW - CORUNNA ROAD and INDUSTRIAL - SOUTH SAGINAW ROUTES

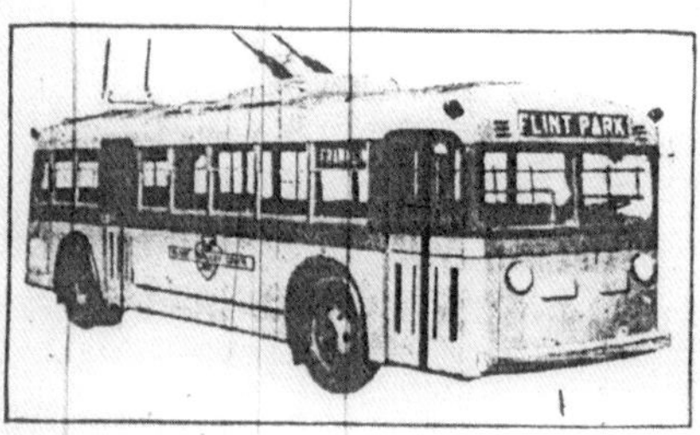

Trolley Coaches Load and Unload at the Curb, Thus Preventing Many Accidents

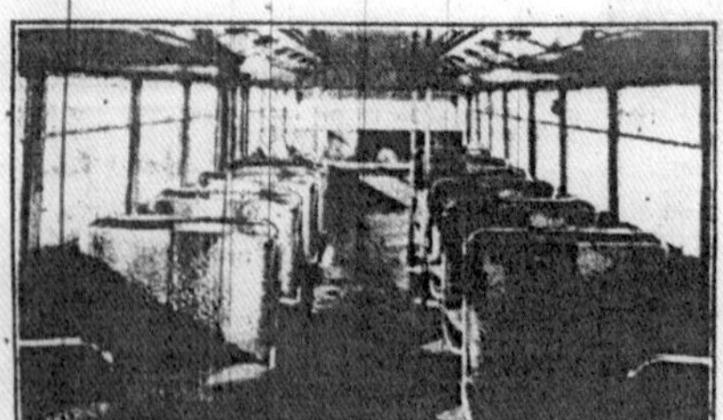

Interiors Are Well Lighted, Seats Comfortable and Aisles Are Wide

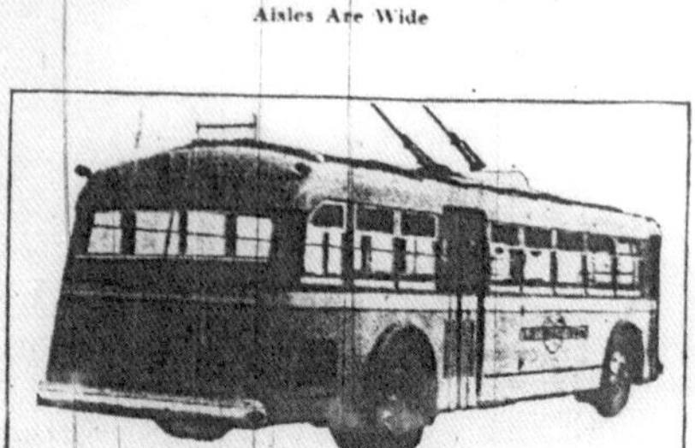

Sleek Looking and Fast

SUNDAY morning, December 6th, the first electric trolley coaches, units in Flint's new co-ordinated transportation system, will make their inaugural trips with 10-minute service on opening day.

The first two routes to obtain this long-awaited, brand-new service will be the North Saginaw-Corunna Road, and South Saginaw-Industrial line, as far as Wager. Trolley wire from Industrial to Flint Park will be completed in a few days.

Thereafter, as rapidly as additional trolley wire is received and hung, the new equipment will go into operation, replacing the gas buses now in use.

While the new equipment will give Flint one of the finest, all-new transportation systems in the country, the rate of fare will be less than is charged in most cities. Ten tickets will be sold for 50 cents, thus giving a five-cent ride. Four tickets can be purchased for 25 cents, two for 15 cents and single fares will remain at 10 cents. Transfers are free, but no stopover is allowed and they must be used on the first coach arriving at the intersecting point of the two lines.

School children can ride for a five-cent cash fare by presenting an identification card which must be obtained from the company office at 13th and S. Saginaw Streets. E. M. R. tickets which are outstanding will be accepted.

THE
FLINT TROLLEY COACH
INC.

An advertisement for the launching of trolley coach service.

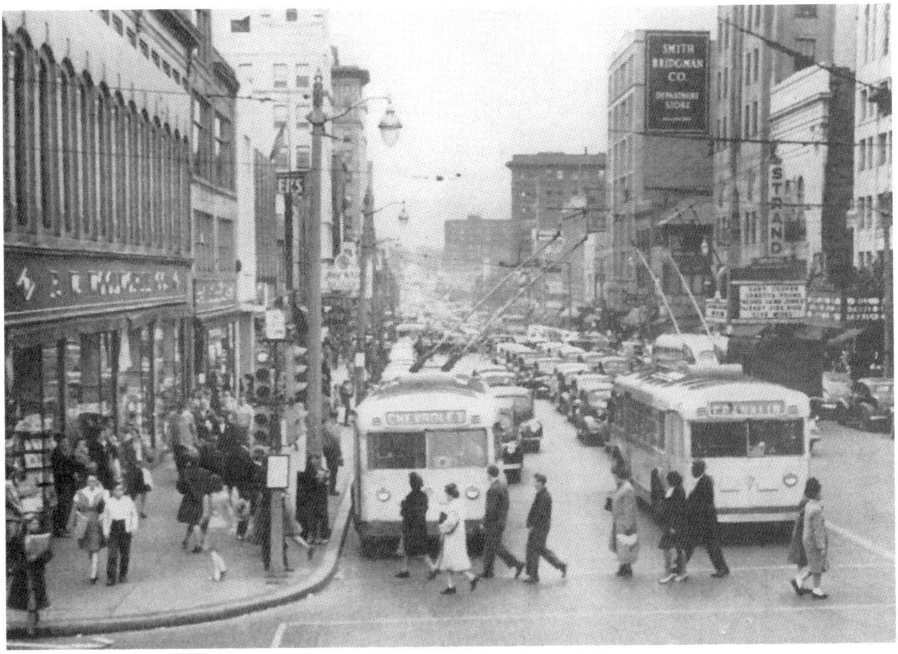

Trolley coaches in downtown Flint.

interurban business. In 1915, the car barns where the streetcars were stored and maintained were built at 1701 South Saginaw at Twelfth Street.

Extensions to the Flint city system grew rapidly up to the year 1920. There were streetcar lines running north on North Saginaw and Detroit Street; south on South Saginaw and Lippincott Boulevard; east on Second Street, Lewis Street, Delaware Avenue and Lapeer Road; and west on Stewart Street, Dayton Street, Third Avenue, West Court Street, Glenwood Avenue and Brown Street. By the time the DUR went into receivership in 1925, Flint had 37.5 miles of track in operation and a fleet of eighty-eight streetcars, some with trailer cars in heavily used routes. When the DUR sought a fare increase, Flint objected. The DUR offered to sell the transit service to the city, but Flint wanted nothing to do with municipal ownership of the transit system. A federal court finally ordered the streetcar fare raised to seven cents by July 30, 1925. Eastern Michigan Railways (EMR) took over the system in 1928. By the early 1930s, the fare had been raised to ten cents.

Interurban service ended between Flint and Saginaw in 1929 and between Flint and Detroit in 1931. In 1932, ten modern cars arrived in

Flint from Pontiac, but they were not enough. Streetcar service ended in Flint on Saturday, April 4, 1936. The final streetcar stopped at 2:30 a.m. early Sunday morning, with a small ceremony by Sheriff Thomas Wolcott, Motorman George Kettler and three sentimental passengers. The following Monday morning, a crew from Flint Scrap Iron & Metal began removing the downtown tracks to prepare for resurfacing.

Streetcars required two motormen to operate and, with the increased automobile traffic, were becoming a safety hazard. The streetcars were temporarily replaced by EMR buses. The newer streetcars in the fleet were sold to a streetcar line in Oklahoma City. The rest were sold or scrapped.

EMR applied for a new franchise, proposing the use of trolley buses, and established a one-mile demonstration line using a borrowed electric coach from Newark, New Jersey. On June 8, 1936, Flint voters approved EMR's proposal for a trolley bus system. EMR changed the name of its Flint transit service to Flint Trolley Coach, Inc., and ordered forty-six yellow coaches with thirty-six seats from General Motors. A system of eight lines and twenty-six route miles was mapped out.

General Motors displayed a new electric trolley coach at the corner of South Saginaw and Kearsley Streets in late November 1936. It was powered by two sixty-five-horsepower electric motors designed so that one could operate the bus if the other one failed. Enough new trolley lines were strung so that trolley coach service formally began on the North Saginaw–Corunna Road route and the portion of the South Saginaw–Industrial Avenue route as far as Wager Avenue on Sunday, December 6, 1936. At 12:17 a.m. that day, dignitaries departed the bus barn at South Saginaw at Twelfth Streets and traveled the North Saginaw route to the end of the line at Carpenter Road, where the trolley coach circled and returned to the barn. Unfortunately, an eighty-seven-day strike forced the buses off the road two days later.

Meanwhile, the city approved a bid by Laro Coal & Iron to purchase the old salvaged streetcar rails for $13.50 per ton. A federally funded Works Progress Administration (WPA) project began removing the rails from the neighborhood streets. Some of the rails were reused in a WPA rail repair project in Detroit.

When the strike was settled on March 5, 1937, full trolley coach service began on four routes: North Saginaw Street–Corunna Road; Flint Park–Industrial Avenue–South Saginaw Street; Detroit Street–Lewis Street–St. John Street; and Civic Park–Franklin Avenue. The gasoline-powered bus routes were Lapeer Road–Flushing Road, Fenton Road–Thrift City (Davison Road) and Fleming Road–Dayton Street. The new trolley lines had two sets of wire, designed to eliminate radio interference, which had been a problem with the old streetcar trolley lines. The trolley buses had two poles attached to the trolley lines and could load passengers curbside, improving passenger safety. The streetcars had stopped in the middle of the street to pick up and drop off passengers.

The golden era of trolley bus service were the World War II years, when gasoline rationing meant that the family car was kept parked most of the time and the buses were used heavily to save on gas. Minor extensions to the trolley lines were made in later years. After World War II, the St. John Street portion of the Lewis Street line was cut.

After the war, additional trolley buses were purchased from ACF–Brill Motors. Forty-four were purchased in 1946, another forty-four in 1947 and forty-six in 1951. Additional route extensions after 1950 used gas and diesel coaches, not trolley coaches. Unfortunately for the bus line, the postwar consumer boom included the purchase of private automobiles, and the GM factories were hard-pressed to expand their parking lots. This caused a considerable drop in bus passengers.

So on Friday, March 23, 1956, the now-renamed Flint City Coach Lines ended trolley bus service and converted to a fleet of diesel-powered coaches, all built by General Motors. Route extensions were also announced. Before power was cut to the trolley lines, a new diesel coach had a mechanical problem, so trolley #875 made one more run than scheduled and discharged its final passenger at 4:40 p.m. The name of the passenger was not recorded, but the final trolley bus driver was Ernest Leffel, a longtime operator for the transit firm. The newer trolley buses in the fleet were sold to the transit system in Winnipeg, Manitoba. The copper trolley lines were sold to the highest bidder and removed. Flint City Coach Lines offered the underground conduit lines to the city for one dollar.

The old barns at South Saginaw and Twelfth Streets were added on to several times over the years and went through several transit company operators, including the current operator, the Mass Transportation Authority. They were torn down after the MTA moved to its present location at 1401 South Dort Highway in 1977.

Today, only Boston, Newark, New Orleans, Philadelphia, Pittsburgh, San Francisco and Toronto still have their streetcar lines, which have been updated to modern light rail systems. These systems have been introduced in other cities, including Detroit with its Downtown People Mover. Many people blame General Motors for the demise of streetcars, as it joined with Standard Oil of California (now Chevron) and Firestone Tires to form National City Lines, which purchased streetcar lines around the country and replaced streetcars with buses. Traffic engineers, many of whom had studied at General Motors Institute (now Kettering University), considered streetcars a traffic hazard. The trolley bus solved the traffic hazard, but only Boston, San Francisco, Seattle and Dayton (Ohio) are operating trolley buses in the United States currently. Dayton almost lost its trolley buses, but they were saved by the 1973 Arab oil embargo, when petroleum was in short supply and Dayton leaders decided that electricity was better. The environmental movement also influenced the revival of trolley buses around the world since they have no exhaust fumes. Trolley buses are still being manufactured by New Flyer, which made the newest diesel buses in the MTA fleet.

Should the overhead trolley lines return to Flint streets? It should be noted that the MTA is working with MOTOTECH, Michigan State University and Kettering University to convert a bus to a hybrid electric system.

Material taken from Mac Sebree and Paul Ward's The Trolley Coach in North America *(1974).*

Update: Since that chapter was written, the Mass Transportation Authority (MTA) began building up a fleet of diesel/electric hybrid buses in 2013, beginning with fifteen buses, with additional buses added to replace older diesel buses. The MTA also has a fleet of buses that run on natural gas and a fleet of Your Ride vehicles that run on propane, along with a few buses that run on hydrogen.

Kearsley Park, Then and Now

A century ago, Flint was undergoing explosive growth. Its population in 1900 was 13,103. In 1910, its population was 38,550, and in 1920, it was 91,600. To accommodate that growth, new subdivisions had to be added. But some of Flint's undeveloped land was on flood plains. Major floods took place in 1904 and 1916. There was a later major flood in 1947. The land alongside Flint's rivers and creeks was prone to flooding, so city leaders determined that much of this land should not be developed but should be parkland. One of these areas was the Gilkey Creek Valley, east of what is now Chavez Drive. That fifty-five-acre area, a one-hundred-year flood plain, was donated to the city by the Windiate-Pierce-Davison Company and became Kearsley Park, established in 1917.

Kearsley Park is one of the city's oldest parks. It was designed by world-renowned Boston landscape architect Warren H. Manning through the patronage of carriage- and automaker J. Dallas Dort. When Kearsley Park Subdivision was platted, Kearsley Park Boulevard was built as a raised roadway with an attractive concrete-arch bridge—designed by Indianapolis bridge engineer Daniel B. Luten—spanning Gilkey Creek, as well as a pedestrian underpass allowing access to both sides of Kearsley Park without crossing the street. Both the original bridge and the underpass are still there today. The Gilkey Creek bed south of Kearsley Park Boulevard was paved and was originally used as a wading pool. While the pavement

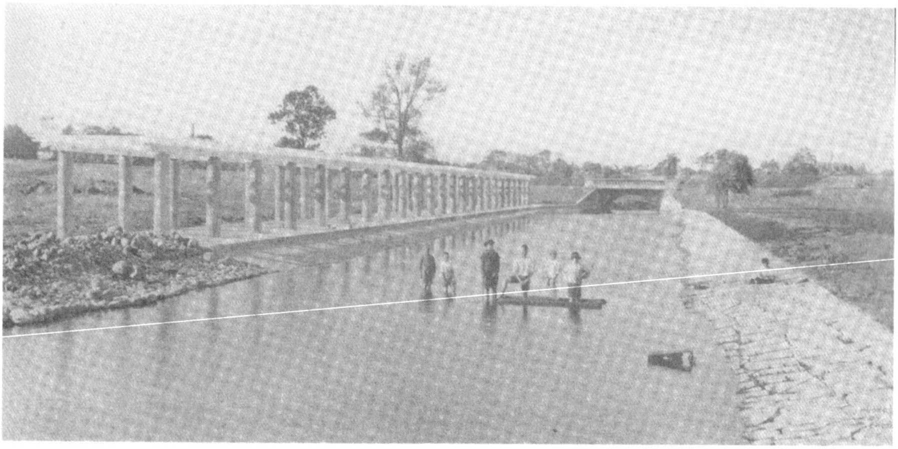

The wading pool at Gilkey Creek, from the 1920 city planning report.

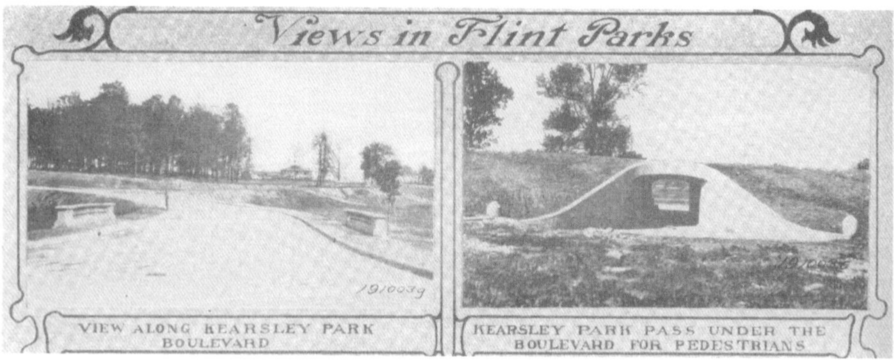

Two views of Kearsley Park Boulevard and the tunnel underneath from the 1920 city planning report.

is still there, you have to look hard to find it; silt and vegetation have built up over time.

Kearsley Park had an outdoor swimming pool, built in 1920, and an adjacent bathhouse and pavilion. The swimming pool was torn down in the late 1960s, as it had become cracked and was too expensive to replace. A playground now stands where the pool once was. The pavilion, now named in honor of the late Genevieve S. Donnelly, was rehabilitated and rededicated in recent years.

In 1963, a miniature village called Safetyville was established by the park board and later operated by the Industrial Mutual Association. It provided drivers' training for elementary school students using small, battery-operated cars the children could drive. Until Riverbank Park opened in 1979, Kearsley Park was the home of the city of Flint's fireworks display on the Fourth of July. The park has always been popular for sledding during the winter months because of its valley terrain. The same terrain also made for a natural amphitheater for occasional concerts. There was a permanent band shell at the park in the 1960s. It was torn down after the city started using portable stages for outdoor concerts in the park.

Until a city air pollution control ordinance enacted in April 1970 prohibited it, Kearsley Park was the home to Flint's traditional "Burning of the Greens" on January 6. After Christmas, the city collected discarded Christmas trees and assembled piles of trees at the park. These piles were then used to create public bonfires in observance of the "Twelfth Night" after Christmas to end the holiday season. On the final Burning of the Greens on January 6, 1970, more than 7,000 trees were burned. In the seventeen years the city held the Burning of the Greens, an estimated 125,000 trees were burned. Trees the city collected after Christmas 1970 went through the chipper.

In the 1970s, city budget cuts caused Kearsley Park's facilities to gradually deteriorate. Safetyville became a target for vandals and was a ghost town by 1980. It was ordered dismantled. With no more fireworks or Burnings of the Greens, people avoided the park, perceiving it as unsafe. That's when the residents rallied to help Kearsley Park, engaging their city councilman, neighboring Mott Community College and the City of Flint to establish the Kearsley Park Partnership.

The partnership sparked a series of improvements to Kearsley Park that began on Earth Day, April 22, 2002. Members of the partnership are the Flint Parks and Recreation Department, the Flint Community Schools, Mott Community College and several neighborhood associations. Phase I of the project involved construction of a barrier-free playground; improvements to the baseball diamond to regulation standards, with dugouts, bleachers and parking, to become the home of Flint Central High School's and Mott Community College's baseball teams; landscaping improvements for the natural amphitheater, including the sledding area; and renovations to the historic pavilion. The pavilion improvements were designed by Wesley Bintz and paid for by a grant from the Department of Natural Resources.

Phase II improvements took place in 2003 with the development of a bicycle and walking path to connect with a countywide bike and pedestrian trail paid for by a grant from the Michigan Department of Transportation.

Today, the Kearsley Park Project organizes park activities under project director Kay Kelly. If J. Dallas Dort were around today, he would be pleased with how the park he spearheaded turned out. It's still a beautiful park.

Thanks to Kearsley Park project director Kay Kelly and Myra Gullett, of the Flint Public Library, who grew up near Kearsley Park. Other material was found in the 1920 Flint city planning report prepared by city planner John Nolen.

Hamady Sacks and Yankee Hats

When I was growing up on Flint's northeast side in the 1960s, the main commercial shopping area in the neighborhood was on Richfield Road. Two local chain stores were located at the corner of Richfield and Center Roads. The Hamady Bros. supermarket was opened on February 11, 1958, and the Yankee Store (selling general merchandise) opened next to the Hamady Bros. store on October 22, 1959. Both Hamady and Yankee were very successful and opened stores outside the Flint area.

Hamady Bros. was a Flint fixture for eighty years. It began in 1911 as a single small store near the Buick factory on Industrial Avenue. It was founded by two Lebanese immigrant cousins, Michael and Kamol Hamady. They pioneered self-service shopping for practical reasons—they knew little English. At a time when customers usually asked for groceries from the clerk, who would then pick them up from the shelves, the Hamady "brothers" (they called themselves brothers to limit customer confusion over their relationship) laid out their products for the customers to select themselves and then give to the clerk to complete the transaction.

As Flint's population grew with the success of Buick automobiles, the Hamadys prospered. Their early deliveries were by horse and buggy, and they did a lucrative business with local farmers. The Hamady reputation was formed early on by offering excellent customer service combined with community involvement. By 1918, Hamady Bros. had grown to eighteen

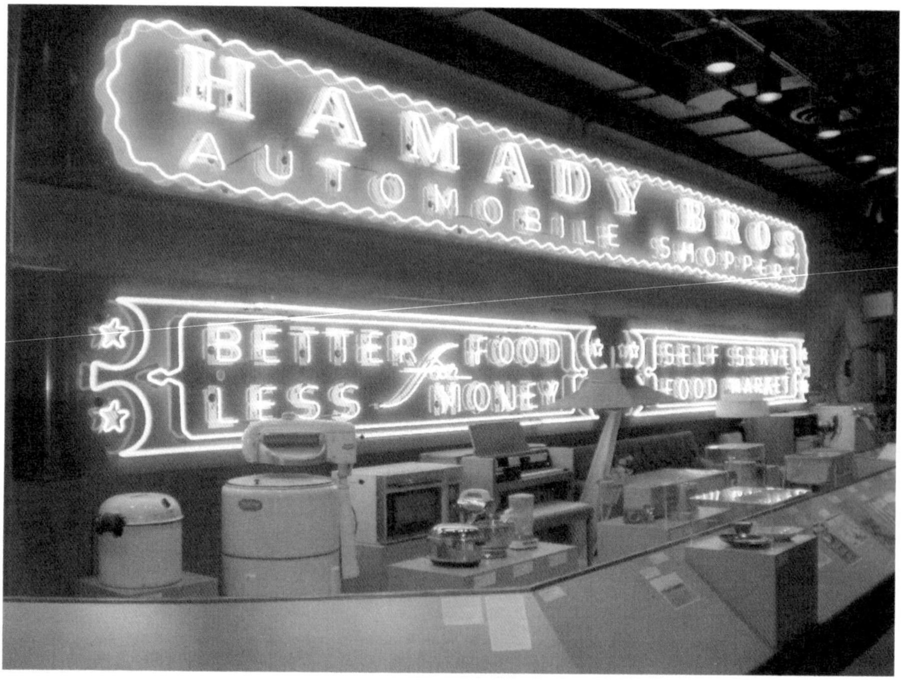

A surviving Hamady Bros. neon sign on display at the Sloan Museum. It came from the location at Davison and Belsay Roads in Burton.

stores throughout Flint. The chain survived the Great Depression and competition from national chains such as A&P. Hamady's reputation was further enhanced during the 1937 sit-down strike when it provided food to the strikers. Hamady's influence on Flint-area shoppers was so great that older Flint shoppers still refer to paper grocery bags as "Hamady sacks."

The forward-thinking Michael Hamady noticed the importance of automobiles and, in the 1940s, began building larger supermarkets with plenty of adjacent parking spaces and neon signs proudly proclaiming, "HAMADY BROS. AUTOMOBILE SHOPPERS FOOD MARKET." Michael's son, Robert, took over the company in 1954. He oversaw the expansion of Hamady Bros., in the 1950s and '60s, into the suburbs and the construction of a large distribution warehouse at 3301 South Dort Highway (the current Security Packaging location). Robert Hamady died in 1967. Kamol Hamady died in 1968, and Michael Hamady died in 1969. Jack A. Hamady (Michael's nephew) became Hamady president in 1967. The 1970s brought about increased competition from A&P, Kroger and K-Mart

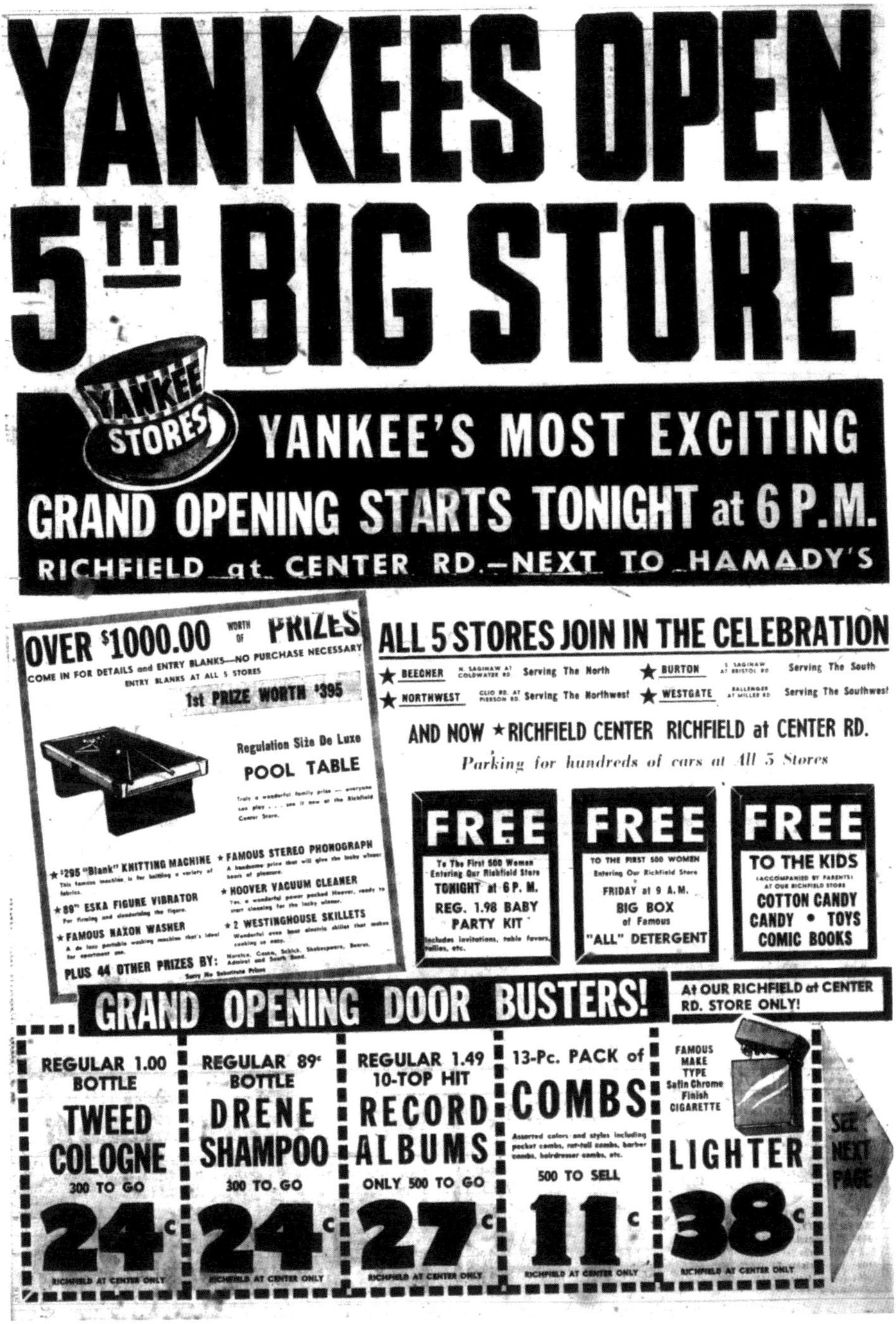

A 1959 grand opening ad for Yankee Stores location on Richfield Road.

Foods. But it was the addition of Meijer into the Flint-area marketplace in 1972 that led the Hamady family to sell out, in 1974, to Durant Enterprises, led by Alex Dandy.

Dandy expanded Hamady into other cities by buying the Saginaw-based Vescio supermarkets and purchasing closed Kroger stores in western and northern Michigan, among other expansions and acquisitions. But additional competition (including a new competitor, former Hamady executive Al Kessel, who opened Kessel Food Markets in former Kroger locations), financial setbacks and Dandy's disputed dealings (which partially led to a seven-week strike by Hamady employees in 1987) shrunk the Hamady chain. It was driven into bankruptcy in November 1987. Federal prosecutors claimed that Dandy ordered kickbacks from suppliers and demanded donations from suppliers to his "Operation Christmas" relief project and then pocketed much of the money. Dandy was convicted in 1992 on tax evasion and fraud charges, fined $5.8 million and sentenced to twenty-three years in federal prison. He was able to reduce his tax liability to $1.1 million and was released after eight years for good behavior. Alex Dandy died on April 21, 2003.

A Hamady supplier, M&B Distributing, led by James McColgan, took control of the Hamady chain on July 19, 1989, and received additional financing to keep it going. But that and concessions by Hamady employees were not enough; the Hamady chain filed Chapter 11 for a second time in May 1991 and closed for good in June 1991. There were accusations that the new Hamady executives profited from questionable business practices. For example, Hamady president Stephen Klein controlled MKM Investments, Inc., which acquired ten of twenty-one Hamady store properties in 1990 and raised annual rents by about $500,000 to more than $1.4 million. The bankruptcy judge approved the sale of Hamady locations on July 3, 1991. Thirteen of the locations were picked up by Kessel, including the Richfield Road location in my old neighborhood that reopened as Kessel on August 25, 1991. M&B itself was sold to Melody Foods on June 1991. That's the Hamady story.

The Yankee Store story is much shorter but very successful. Yankee was founded in 1948 in downtown Flint as U.S. Surplus Sales by partners Joseph Megdell and Wilbert Roberts. They started out together in a scrap metal business on North Dort Highway before opening the army surplus store and renaming the new retailing venture Yankee Stores. Advertising heavily and capitalizing on what Megdell called a postwar hunger for merchandise, the Yankee Stores expanded into twenty-one stores within nineteen years. Besides Flint, Yankee Stores were located in Davison, Saginaw, Bay City, Lansing, East Lansing, Pontiac, Owosso, Mt. Pleasant, Albion and Midland by 1964. The eighteen stores Yankee operated that year had fourteen hundred employees, a $3.25 million payroll and grossed $35 million annually. Most of the Yankee Stores were supermarket-sized general merchandise stores selling hard and soft goods, including small appliances. They were often located next to grocery stores such as Hamady, which enjoyed a close business relationship with Yankee in the Flint area, hence the adjacent Hamady Bros. and Yankee Stores on Richfield Road (which also had a Citizens Bank branch). Not quite one-stop shopping, but you could do your banking at Citizens, do your grocery shopping at Hamady Bros. next door and get the rest of the things you needed at Yankee.

In 1961, Yankee opened its first big box location, dubbed "Yankee Stadium Store," in the Northwest Shopping Center (now Hallwood Plaza), at the corner of Clio and Pierson Roads. For the grand opening of the 108,000-square-foot store, Megdell brought in Norm Cash and Frank Lary of the Detroit Tigers, Whitey Ford and Elston Howard of the New York Yankees and veteran sports announcer and former Detroit Tigers broadcaster Van Patrick. (Patrick was replaced in 1960 by Ernie Harwell due to a change in sponsors for Tiger broadcasts.) They attracted quite a crowd. A second Yankee Stadium Store opened in 1964 at the former Dort Drive-In Theatre location, at the corner of South Dort Highway and Atherton Road, as the first store in the Dort Mall. In 1965, Megdell and Roberts sold the Yankee Store chain to Detroit-based Borman Foods, which ran the Farmer Jack supermarket chain.

A preview of what was to come came when Megdell attended the first Borman Foods board meeting after selling Yankee Stores to Borman. Megdell had ideas about running Yankee, and old man Borman said, "You did not buy us out. We bought you out." Megdell remained president until he retired in 1967. Not long after Megdell's departure, the chain began a gradual decline. Borman Foods moved Yankee's base of operations from Flint to Detroit and sold the Yankee distribution warehouse on East Court Street near South Dort Highway to the Flint Board of Education. The board needed a new location for its warehouse, as its old one was in the path of the I-475 expressway. I remember when my parents took me to the warehouse clearance sale at the vacating Yankee warehouse, and I recall they bought glassware there.

The decline of Yankee Stores under Borman Foods (which concentrated on replacing the smaller stores with big-box Yankee Department Stores) was hastened by an unsuccessful expansion into the Detroit marketplace, where there was plenty of competition at K-Mart's home base. By 1971, Borman Foods had closed the Detroit-area Yankee Department Stores and sold the out-state Michigan stores on February 1972 to the New York–based Hartfield-Zodys discount store chain. Borman should have realized that selling cuts of meat is not done the same way as selling electric shavers. Hartfield-Zodys phased out the remaining small-format Yankee Stores (including the Richfield Road location) and renamed the remaining Yankee Department Stores as Zodys. It also built additional Zodys stores to replace the closed Yankee Stores, including a new Zodys at Davison Road near Belsay Road in Burton (where there was also a Hamady store). But the 1973 Arab oil embargo and the resulting recession forced Hartfield-Zodys to file for Chapter 11 bankruptcy protection on November 1974, and the first thing it did was to close the Michigan stores.

The Store Closing Sale began at the Michigan Zodys stores on November 27, 1974, and I believe the stores were all closed by the end of the year, thus ending the final chapter of the history of the Yankee Store chain. The Davison Road Zodys later housed a Harley-Davidson motorcycle dealership, which has since moved. Throughout most of the history of Yankee Stores, the store's symbol has been Uncle Sam's red, white and blue hat. There was a time in the 1960s when the Yankee Stores chain could have been the Walmart of the North, when Megdell and Roberts were running the company. All it had to do was concentrate on Michigan's small and medium-sized cities, similar to what Sam Walton did when he built the Walmart chain, starting with smaller southeastern American cities and expanding from there.

Back at Richfield Road, the closed Yankee store remained vacant for about four years before Hamady decided to renovate and expand in 1976, absorbing the closed Yankee store space and doubling the size of the Hamady Complete Food Center. When Kessel bought the closed Hamady stores, it quickly changed the signs and repainted the interiors before reopening the stores as Kessel stores. Because of the large size of the Richfield Road Kessel store, I would have thought it would give that store a serious remodeling.

Kroger bought twenty Kessel locations, including the Richfield Road one, in December 1999. Kroger originally planned on operating as Kessel in the Flint, Saginaw and Bay City TV market before deciding to gradually phase out the Kessel name in favor of Kroger.

The Richfield Road store's turn for major renovation took place in 2003, when Citizens Bank vacated the Richfield Center branch to make room for additional supermarket space that included a new pharmacy drive-thru window and a new loading dock. During the renovation, I did a little amateur archaeology at the store when the suspended ceiling panels were removed, revealing the original plaster ceiling for both Hamady and Yankee. The workmen didn't bother removing the old fluorescent fixtures before putting up the suspended ceiling, and the old Hamady ceiling has nicely colored, detailed plaster cornice work still hidden by the new suspended ceiling at the beautifully renovated Kroger store. While Hamady and Yankee are long gone, Citizens Bank is still going strong as the largest bank holding company based in Michigan. As for the former Yankee Stadium Stores, most of the Hallwood Plaza location is now occupied by Kroger. At the Dort Mall, the space was subdivided, and the bulk of it is used by Bargain Hunterz, Perani's Hockey Shop and a bingo hall.

If you go to the Sloan Museum in the Cultural Center, there is a permanent exhibit on Flint's past that includes reminders of the Yankee and Hamady stores and is dominated by a restored Hamady Bros. neon sign from the Davison and Belsay Roads store.

Thanks to Michael Dandy and David Megdell.

Flint's Own Brand of Soda Pop

At the end of the 1991 film *Fried Green Tomatoes*, you can see, among the many metal advertising signs on the closed Whistle Stop Café, an M&S Beverages sign. The irony of that scene is that M&S was never available outside of Michigan, bootleg shipments to transplanted Michiganians notwithstanding. M&S was marketed in the Flint, Saginaw and Thumb areas, not Juliette, Georgia, where the movie was filmed.

Charles Weinstein got asked about M&S every time someone he knew saw the movie, or so it seemed. His father, Morris Weinstein, co-founded M&S with Samuel Buckler. It's assumed that M&S stood for Morris and Samuel. But Charles Weinstein insisted that M&S stood for "moon and stars." Later on, M&S would also stand for "mellow and smooth," as well as "Michigan's Supreme."

Morris Weinstein arrived in the United States from Poland about a century ago. He worked in Detroit for the Feigenson brothers' soft drink company, which would become Faygo. Moving to Flint in 1918, he partnered with Buckler, who also worked for the Feigensons, to form the Independent Bottling Works at Eighth Street, near Saginaw Street. They bottled strawberry, grape and lime sodas, as well as Hires Root Beer. During Prohibition, the company provided malt for home brewers of near beer. It was around that time that the bottling company was renamed M&S, inspired by the label and celestial logo for K&M Malt (which the company offered).

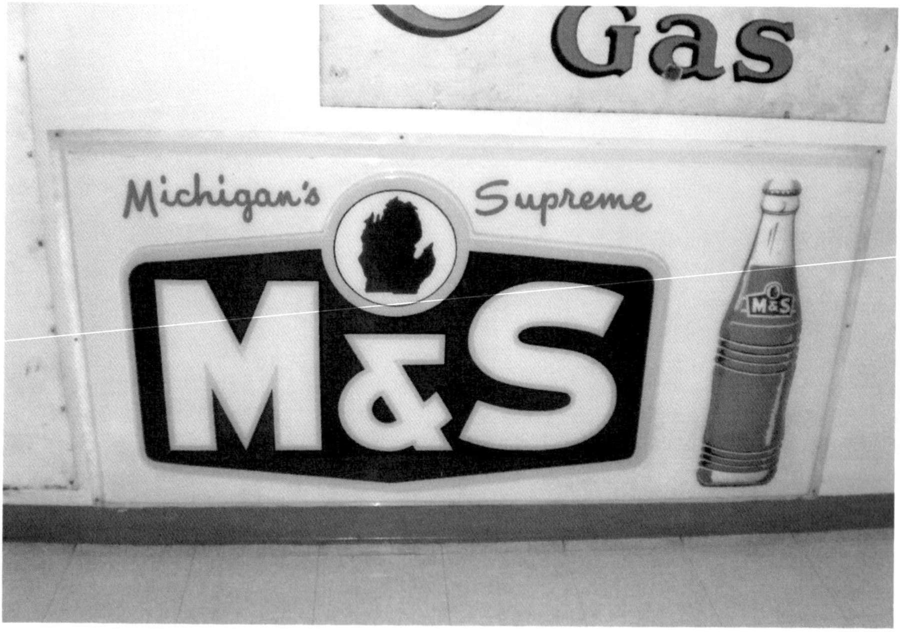

An M&S sign found in the Dort Mall.

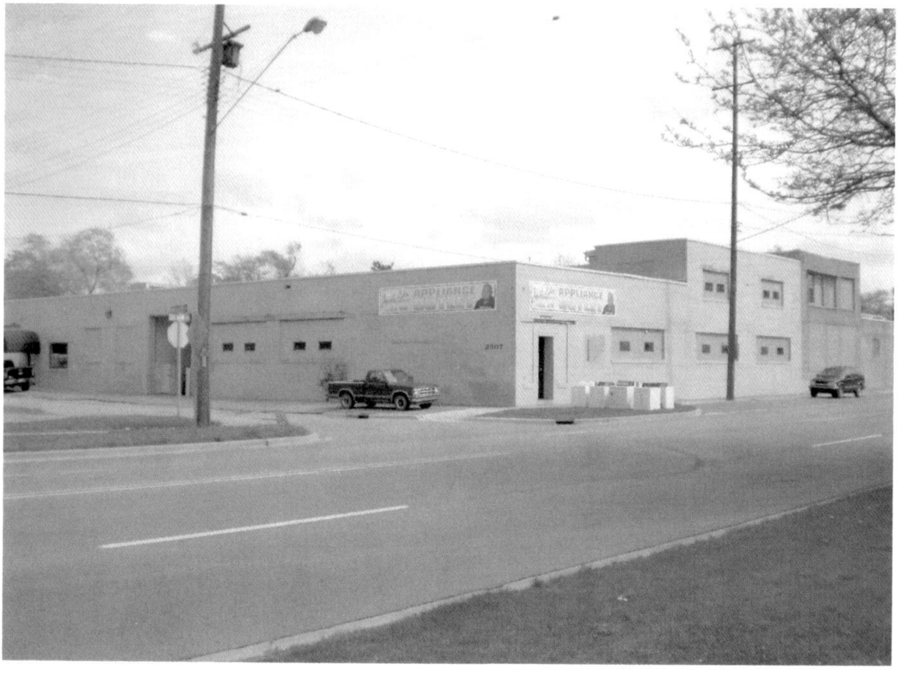

The former M&S Beverages plant on South Saginaw, now a used appliance store.

Morris Weinstein died in 1938. In 1944, the Weinstein family bought out Buckler's interest in the company. Samuel Buckler would establish Buckler Beverage, taking the Hires franchise with him. The Buckler Beverage plant was located at 2603 Lapeer Road next to the Coca-Cola bottling plant. Buckler Beverage also bottled Squirt and Crush, among other franchised soda brands, until it folded in 1981. Samuel Buckler died in 1972. The old plant was torn down in 1997 to make room for the new sales and distribution warehouse addition to the Coca-Cola plant.

During World War II, M&S was also producing Dr Pepper, which, because of sugar rationing, became advantageous; Dr Pepper used half the amount of sugar as Hires Root Beer. Later on, M&S would produce Canada Dry products. About 1961, M&S acquired the Seven Up Bottling Company of Flint and started bottling Seven Up at the M&S plant at 2307 South Saginaw Street. M&S also bottled Mason's Root Beer and Wolverine Ginger Ale at that time. The various flavors M&S offered changed over the years, but the popular flavors were orange and strawberry-cherry, which started in Flint. Customers called strawberry-cherry soda "red pop," so M&S put the name "red pop" on the label. Ironically, Feigenson said in the late 1950s that red pop was cheapening the product even though Faygo started using the name itself two years later. Charles Weinstein recalled handing out bottles of red pop on Halloween.

The local Hamady Bros. supermarket chain noticed that shoppers were mixing bottles in the M&S cartons and suggested that M&S produce a variety pack of flavors. This package was a big seller.

By the time the Weinstein family sold M&S Beverage Company to Universal Foods of Milwaukee in 1969, the size of the bottles had gradually increased from seven to sixteen ounces. M&S also sold its beverages in individual quart bottles. Universal Foods would eventually follow the rest of the soft drink industry in producing products in disposable bottles. But when Michigan voters approved a bottle deposit law in 1976, Universal Foods decided to move the Seven Up/M&S bottling plant from its longtime Saginaw Street home to a larger location in the former Arlan's Department Store at G-2051 West Bristol Road at Van Slyke Road. It moved into the new plant just in time, as the bottle deposit law went into effect in 1978. As part of the renovation, the concrete slab floor was replaced by a thicker floor to accommodate bottling equipment and delivery trucks.

While the company, which became Mid-Continent Bottlers under Universal Foods, still sold M&S flavors, it dropped M&S Orange to produce Sunkist Orange soda. While it bottled Dr Pepper for distribution in Saginaw, Buckler Beverage had the Flint rights, so when Buckler Beverage folded, Mid-Continent picked up the Flint rights to Dr Pepper. It also distributed Vernors, Royal Crown Cola, Diet-Rite Cola and A&W Root Beer, all of which were bottled by Vernors in Detroit. The Flint plant came in handy during a labor dispute at Vernors in 1982, as Vernors management made arrangements with Mid-Continent Bottlers to produce Vernors products during the Vernors strike. When Vernors shut down its Detroit bottling plant in 1985, the Seven Up/M&S plant picked up the Vernors, RC and Diet-Rite franchises.

The Flint plant and Saginaw distribution warehouse went through several ownership changes in the 1980s. Seven Up's parent company at that time, Philip Morris, acquired the Seven Up Bottling Company of Flint in 1984, and the bottle caps began to read, "Sevco Beverage," instead of Mid-Continent Bottlers. Shortly afterward, in 1985, headlines were made when three African American partners, car dealers Al Bennett and Mel Farr (the former Detroit Lions star) and Detroit attorney Charles Wells, bought the bottling company. It became the Bennett, Farr and Wells Bottling Company, with the caps saying "BFW Bottling Company, Flint, MI." Unfortunately, the small bottling company could not effectively compete with the larger Coke and Pepsi bottlers, so it was not a big moneymaker for the three partners, who sold the company back to Philip Morris in 1987. In 1988, Philip Morris sold the BFW Bottling Company to Brooks Beverages of Holland, Michigan.

Brooks fired the entire sales, marketing and delivery staff (as it already had a distribution warehouse in Davison) and shut down the Saginaw warehouse (it also had a distribution warehouse in Bay City from which it could send trucks to Saginaw). Brooks did keep the Flint bottling plant going but discontinued the M&S brand because it had its own Sunglo brand of flavors. Just a few days after buying the Flint plant and closing the Saginaw warehouse, it bought the Seven Up Bottling Company of Detroit and shut down the Detroit bottling plant. The Flint plant then produced sixteen-ounce glass bottles of beverages (bottles moved from Detroit) for distribution in both Flint and Detroit. I wish I had kept a sixteen-ounce Vernors bottle with a printed-on label from that time as they were all in mint condition, despite being several years old. Brooks had planned on upgrading the Bristol Road bottling plant, but a surprise consumer shift away from glass bottles in favor of cans and plastic bottles led it to shut down the Flint plant in 1989, and from that point on, the beverages were shipped from the Holland plant, thus closing the final chapter in the M&S Beverage story.

Today, the former plant at 2307 South Saginaw Street is owned by Durant Enterprises and occupies the office area. Most of the plant space is occupied by a used major appliance store with part of the rear portion occupied by a Better Made Potato Chips distribution warehouse. Durant Enterprises uses the upstairs area for storage. A portion of the former Bristol Road plant was used by Brooks (now absorbed into the Dr Pepper/Snapple Bottling Group) as a distribution warehouse for several years, until it and the Bay City warehouse were consolidated into a newly built warehouse north of Flint, at 7300 Exchange Parkway just off the I-75 Mt. Morris Road exit. Great Lakes Recycling now occupies the former Bristol Road plant.

But just like the moon and stars, memories of the cold, refreshing taste of the various flavors of M&S pop will continue to shine brightly. Reminders of M&S can be found in at least three places. In the Sloan Museum, under the Hamady Bros. neon sign, you can see a quart bottle of M&S Straw-Cherry Soda encased in Plexiglas next to a Paramount Potato Chips tin. Near the bottle, you will find an M&S metal sign and a photo of an M&S display inside a Hamady Bros. supermarket, all from the 1950s. You can also find an old M&S metal sign next to the men's room door at the Cracker Barrel Old Country Store and Restaurant on I-75 at the Pierson Road exit as well as a large M&S plastic sign plus a metal sign inside the Dort Mall on South Dort Highway and Atherton Road.

This chapter is dedicated to the memory of Charles Weinstein, who died in 2010. Thanks to Michael Dandy of Durant Enterprises, Charles B. White and the late Charles Weinstein.

Durand Union Station, Then and Now

Southwest of Flint, Amtrak train passengers unfamiliar with the area may be surprised that the small city of Durand has a large, picturesque and historic depot. It was built in 1905 to replace a similar depot that was destroyed by fire. The original depot, dedicated on October 1, 1903, was the subject of the most famous photograph of the depot. The depot was surrounded by seven passenger trains. Facing the camera on the upper left is the Day Express #9 from Port Huron to Chicago. On the other track, going the opposite direction, is the eastbound #2, the Battle Creek–Port Huron Local. At the lower part of the picture, the train at the lower left is #12, the Detroit Express, eastbound from Grand Haven. Ahead of that train, alongside the station, is the Steamboat Express, also headed to Detroit. On the other track, going westbound, is the #19 from Detroit to Grand Haven. Behind the station are two trains facing each other on the same track. On the left is Ann Arbor Railroad train #2 headed for Toledo. On the right, alongside the far side of the station, is Grand Trunk Railway #33, bound for Saginaw and Bay City. One of those two trains would need to back up to a siding to let the other train through.

The original depot was constructed in the Château Revival architectural style, with Missouri granite brick, Bedford cut stone and a slate roof. Inside, the interior had marble wainscoting on the ground floor and oak woodwork. It contained a ticket office, waiting rooms, a ladies' parlor, a gentlemen's

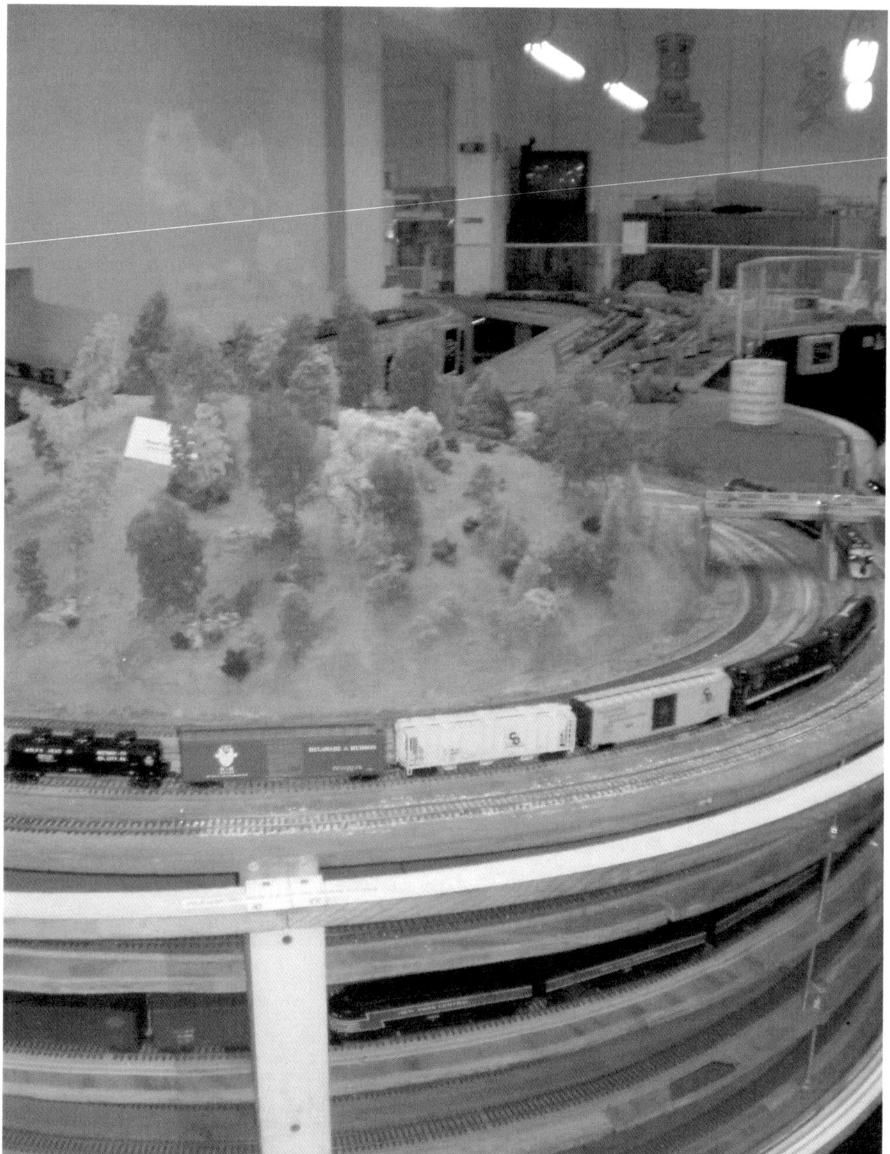

The Durand Model Railroad Club at Union Station.

smoking room, large corridors and a handsome dining room with "all the necessary appurtenances." In the second story, there were offices for the general officials of the western division, dispatchers, operators, sleeping quarters for personnel and Western Union telegraph offices, all heated by steam. The cost of the structure was $60,000 back in 1903.

Yes, with six railroad lines converging on Durand, it became a major rail hub, with the railroad becoming the reason for the town's existence. Five of the lines leading to Chicago, Muskegon (with a car ferry to Milwaukee), Bay City, Canada (via Port Huron) and Detroit were operated by the Grand Trunk Western Railroad. A line to Toledo was run by the Ann Arbor Railroad.

Less than two years after the station was built, it was destroyed by fire, on April 17, 1905. The station was quickly rebuilt, and the new station opened on September 25, 1905. The only change on the outside was the style of the dormers on the red tile roof. It was described in 1905 as a finer and more handsome structure than the former one and better adapted to the needs of the company. Again, the station has gray marble wainscoting, beautiful oak woodwork and a terrazzo floor.

The Durand Union Station would be the hub of bustling activity for the next half century, as trains were the primary means of intercity transportation. The 1900s was the peak time for the railroad industry. In just a single day during that time, forty-two passenger trains, twenty-two mail trains and seventy-eight freight trains would pass through Durand. As many as three thousand passengers used the Durand Depot each day at that time. In 1911, half the population of Durand was employed by the Grand Trunk Western Railroad. Rail traffic declined gradually during the 1920s, when automobiles became popular.

In 1960, the Grand Trunk dropped passenger train service between Durand and Muskegon via Grand Rapids. In 1971, the new national passenger train service, Amtrak, took over passenger train service from the private railroad companies, and the Durand Depot lost passenger trains temporarily. On September 13, 1974, passenger trains returned to Durand as the Amtrak Blue Water Limited began its run between Chicago and Port Huron. But that same year, Grand Trunk determined it could no longer justify the cost of maintaining the huge train station and abandoned it. A trailer was set up to serve Amtrak passengers in the depot's parking lot. The depot seemed doomed, but it was too important a landmark for the people of Durand to see demolished like the roundhouse was in 1961. The community

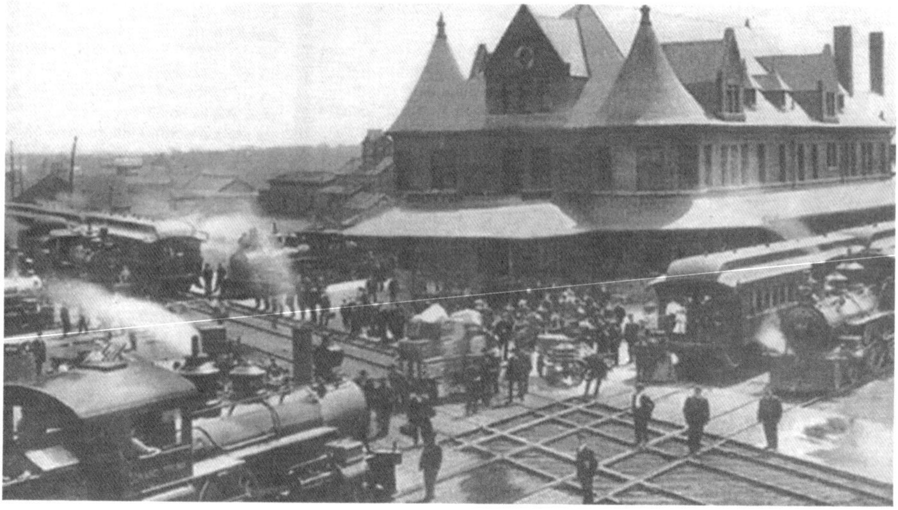

An April 1904 photo of the original Durand Union Station.

rallied to save the station, and in 1979, the City of Durand purchased it from the Grand Trunk Railroad for one dollar. In February 1980, the old depot became an Amtrak station again. Fundraising began to gradually restore the Durand Depot, a project that is still ongoing. The depot received a big boost on Christmas Day 1990, when the State of Michigan announced that the depot would become the home of the Michigan State Railroad History Museum and Information Center. The museum was established inside the former dining room of the depot and shares space with the depot's gift shop. Also on the first floor is a model railroad club.

As you walk around the station, you can see individual names inscribed on granite and embedded in the sidewalks; these are the names of people who donated funds to help restore the depot. The installation of an elevator next to the men's room allowed for restoration and development of the depot's second floor. The second floor contains offices, small museums dedicated to the Ann Arbor and Grand Trunk Western Railroads and a large ballroom in the former sleeping quarters.

The biggest challenge the operators of the Durand Union Station faced took place in January 2009, when a pipe burst in the attic. Both the Durand fire department and Union Station staff arrived within ten minutes. After the pipe burst was reported in the news, I visited Union Station to survey the damage. Hardest hit were the library archives and the model railroad club. The ballroom was occupied by several tables with archive material laid out for drying. The building and contents were fully insured, and there was no permanent damage to archive material. After a year of repairs, the refurbished Union Station had its grand reopening in February 2010.

Today, two Amtrak trains stop at the depot for the Blue Water Limited. The westbound train departs from Durand at 7:47 a.m. headed to Chicago, and the eastbound train departs at 10:14 p.m. headed to Port Huron. Unfortunately, you cannot buy your ticket at the quaint ticket window inside the station, but you can use the Quik-Trak self-service ticketing kiosk on the other side of the waiting room.

Thanks to the staff of Durand Union Station.

Durant Hotel, Then and Now

The year is 1920. Flint is a growing city. Its population has grown from 38,500 in 1910 to 91,600. The man credited with creating this growth was General Motors (GM) founder William C. Durant. Mr. Durant pledged $300,000 for the construction of a hotel that would bear his name. Unfortunately for Mr. Durant, before the hotel opened its doors, he was forced to resign. He lost control of GM during a brief economic downturn and lost a fortune trying to prop up GM's stock price.

The three-hundred-room Durant Hotel opened on December 14, 1920, at 607 East Second Avenue. Each hotel room had its own private bathroom. The first guest to register at the hotel was Michigan governor Albert E. Sleeper. The first event to take place at the hotel was a convention of over one hundred men who were Dort Motor Company dealers and distributors. The hotel offered both Flint residents and visitors a hostelry on par with the hotels of larger American cities in regards to construction, furnishings, decorations and service. Occupying an entire city block downtown, everything about the hotel oozed class. The lobby had large, round onyx columns with a marble tile floor. It was furnished with mahogany davenports and lounge chairs upholstered with overstuffed tapestry covering. It was at once picturesque and serviceable. Up above were six chandeliers of bronze and white opaque crystal glass.

The main dining room was a harmony of silver and blue. The grill was called the *A-do-wa* room, an Indian term meaning satisfaction. Three richly

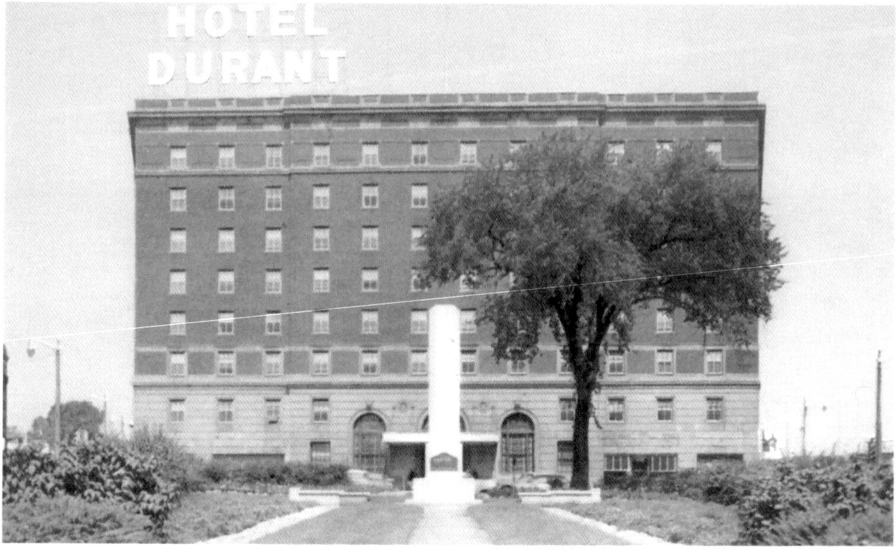

A vintage postcard of the Durant Hotel.

furnished private dining rooms were called the Italian Room, the Louis XIV and the Jacobean. A club room in the basement was used for association and fraternity luncheons. The beautiful ballroom was cheerful in its decoration of old rose hangings and had a spring floor on a concrete foundation.

Over the next fifty years, the hotel was the most prestigious place to stay, dine, hold meetings and stage various social and business gatherings. It was the place for politicians and entertainers to stay while in Flint. On the surface, all seemed well. But underneath, things were not very stable.

There was stability early on. The original operator of the hotel was United Hotel Co. A 130-room addition to the rear of the hotel was completed in 1928. In 1929, United Hotels merged with the Bowman-Biltmore group to create one of the largest hotel operators in the country. This seemed to help the Durant weather the Great Depression. But a circa 1930 renovation of the hotel rooms did not return its investment. The lingering Depression slowed down hotel traffic. The owners fell behind in making mortgage payments to Metropolitan Life Insurance Company, which purchased the hotel at auction in August 1940 as a result of foreclosure proceedings.

Meanwhile, labor problems became nasty as rival labor organizations—the American Federation of Labor (AFL) and the Congress of Industrial Organizations (CIO)—had a jurisdictional dispute. The AFL represented

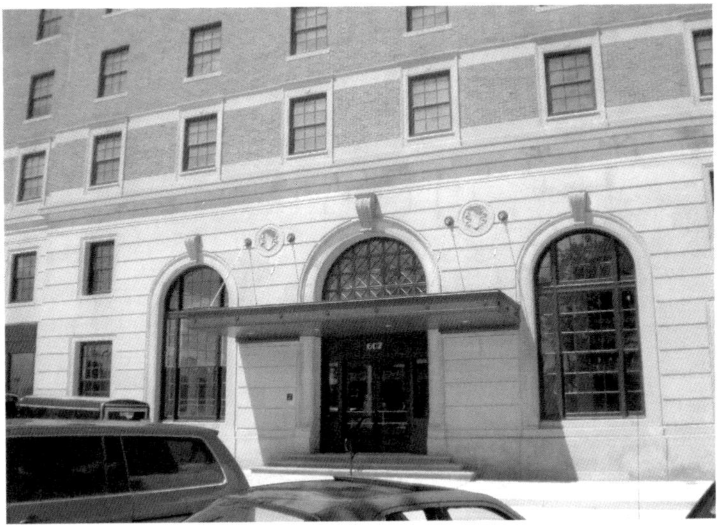

The Durant's restored front entrance.

restaurant workers, while the CIO was trying to organize. It got so bad that a fight developed between a chef and a CIO organizer. This led to the stabbing death of the organizer early in December 1941. The organizer pulled the knife from his wound and stabbed the chef with it before he died. The chef survived and was acquitted on the second-degree murder charge. This was the kind of publicity the Durant Hotel did not need.

A new management contract was granted by Metropolitan Life to Albert Pick Hotels Corp. of Chicago. About $250,000 was spent to rehabilitate the rooms. Upon the Pick Hotel chain assuming ownership of the hotel in June 1942, it was officially renamed the Pick-Durant Hotel. Under Pick management, the hotel became a very efficient operation. Credit has to be given to Scott Shattuck, who managed the hotel from 1944 until his death in 1965. To give an example, the ballroom was gutted in a 1960 fire a week before a scheduled Buick sales force convention. Shattuck hired the Benson Construction Co. to make repairs and refurbish the ballroom; this was completed just in time for the convention. In the 1960s, a high-profile tenant, WNEM-TV channel 5, operated its Flint sales office, news bureau and a small studio at the hotel.

When new lodging developed in the out-county areas in the 1960s with the completion of the I-75 and U.S. 23 expressways, new rivals to the old hotel developed. Examples of new lodging developments in the 1960s were the Howard Johnson Motor Lodge on Miller Road (later Best Western Mister Gibby's Inn, since demolished), the Holiday Inn on Bristol Road

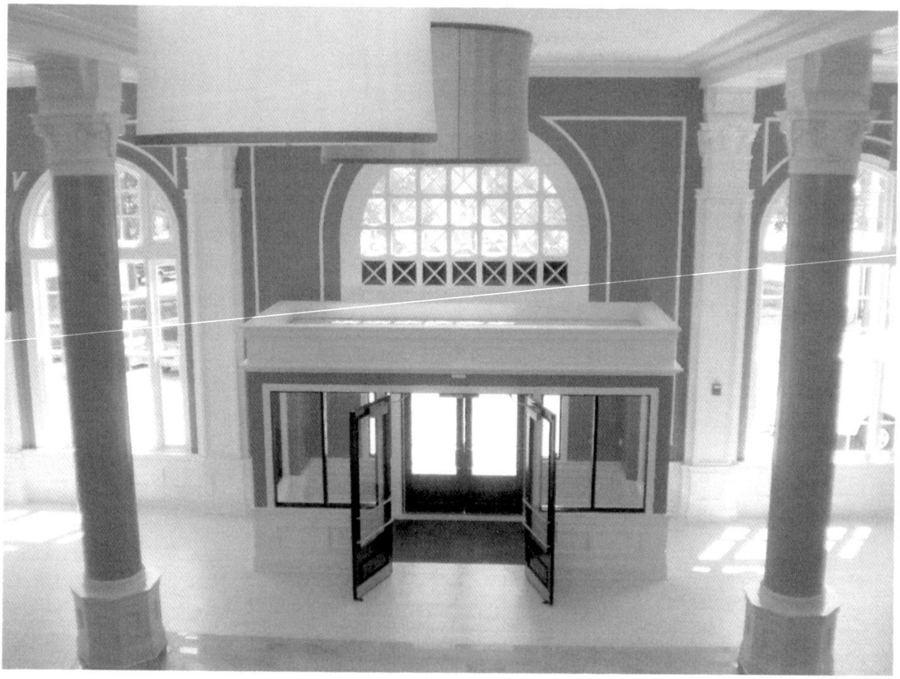

The Durant's restored lobby.

(later Days Inn, now closed) and the Sheraton Inn on Pierson Road (later Ramada Inn, now closed), all located alongside I-75. As early as 1968, there was talk of putting the Pick-Durant Hotel, with its 254 rooms at that time, on the market. There was also talk of converting the hotel into a training school or senior housing, among other uses.

In 1969, Pick settled that issue by announcing that the hotel would be completely remodeled. The renovation cost was estimated at $1.5 million. The lobby was redesigned and refurbished, the floor space was revamped to create two new restaurants, executive suites were created, the exterior was upgraded (including the replacement of electric signs), parking was expanded and all the rooms were redecorated for the renamed Pick-Durant Motor Hotel. My father, who was a plasterer, worked on the renovation and picked up old hotel furniture in the process, including a desk and a headboard, which I still have.

While the 1971 convention business did boost downtown activity, the renovations were not enough. The flight to the suburbs continued the decline of downtown Flint. On December 31, 1972, Pick Hotels announced that the hotel would be put up for sale. There were no buyers. Things were not looking good in July 1973, when the Flint City Club vacated the hotel because the lease expired. Three arson fires were reported at the hotel in 1973. At the end of August, Pick announced that the hotel would close if there was no buyer. On September 29, the windows of the hotel's Royal Scots Grill were boarded up. The following day, the hotel closed. One of the last guests to check out was Mrs. Madge Surtees Hale. She was a former actress who was a dining room hostess at the hotel and had lived there since 1950.

Many of Flint's business leaders in 1973 thought that the hotel would not stay vacant for long. It was said that the property, almost an acre in size and occupying most of the block bounded by Second and Third (now University) Avenues and North Saginaw and Detroit (now M.L. King) Streets, was too commercially valuable to stand empty for any length of time. It was thought at the time that the most logical choice would be continued use as a hotel or inn with the expected development of the University of Michigan–Flint downtown campus.

In the more than thirty years since the hotel closed, nothing was done. Pick Hotels stripped the Pick-Durant of furnishings, which were sent to its other hotels in 1974. The Flint Sheraton Inn acquired the hotel's bar about 1977. There have been several proposals for the hotel over the years that included apartments, condominiums, senior citizens' housing or other forms of housing, as well as a Job Corps Center. The most promising proposal over the years was a conversion to senior housing in 1980; this proposal was dashed when the city council refused to guarantee a federal loan to help fund the proposal. In the first few years after its closing, ghosts of the hotel showed up when the old Motor Hotel neon sign continued to light up at night and the phone number remained listed in the phone book in 1979. But soon the phone number was disconnected and the neon sign was taken down. A beautiful female ghost was reported in the hotel in 1979. In 2005, trees grew on the hotel's roofs. Many of the upstairs windows were broken.

A Texas firm purchased the hotel in 1976. In 1980, the owner owed $75,677.00 in back taxes. In 1993, the closed hotel was purchased in a tax sale by Kumar Vemulapalli. He donated the building to Odyssey House in 1995. Odyssey House tried for years to get a package together to rehabilitate the building, but it never happened. On May 10, 2005, Odyssey House completed the sale of the hotel to Alfred Kloss, owner of Daystar Development, which owns the Dryden, Ferris, Old Genesee Bank and Universal Buildings downtown. The legal owner was Flint Renaissance Group, Inc., with the same address as Daystar Development in the Dryden Building. The asking price when it was listed in 2004 was $301,000.00. The recorded sale price was $51,956.58. The 2005 State Equalized Value of the building was $51,700.00. Considering the condition of the building, some people believed the best option was demolition, which was estimated to cost $8,000.00 in 2005. It was reported that Kloss was working with a developer, but Kloss sold the hotel later that year to the Genesee County Land Bank for over $200,000.00, with the money coming from the Mott Foundation. On October 28, 2008, the pieces finally fell in place for the Durant Hotel to be renovated in a $30 million project to convert the hotel rooms into ninety-three residential apartments. The renovated building would be called The Durant.

The contractors for the project are two Lansing-based developers, Karp & Associates and Prater Development. I toured The Durant with Kevin Prater of Prater Development. It turned out to be a total gut job. A later kitchen addition was torn down, and a parking structure was built behind the old hotel. The lobby and ballroom were restored to their former glory. The Tennessee Marble Company mentioned that its marble was used on its stairways. Much of it survived and was relocated to the center of the lobby floor within the four Corinthian columns that rise to the second-story ceiling. In the ballroom, the checkerboard-pattern mosaic tile floor survived surprisingly intact.

The apartments are spacious, with modern appliances and fantastic views of the city. Even though the units were not ready for occupancy until August 2010, 25 percent were already leased in June.

With the renovation, the State Equalized Value in 2009 was $222,000 and jumped to $1.6 million in 2010. Nearby, Witherbee's Market opened at the corner of M.L. King (formerly Detroit Street) and University Avenue (formerly Third Avenue). This is the first grocery store to be located in downtown Flint in decades and gives tenants of The Durant a convenient place to shop. The Durant has become yet another desirable place to live downtown, following First Street Lofts, Wade Trim, Berridge Place, the Rowe Building, the University of Michigan–Flint dormitory and Riverfront Student Housing at the former Hyatt Regency Hotel.

Thanks to Kraemer Design Group and Kevin Prater of Prater Development.

Remembering Flint Central High School

Budget problems and shrinking enrollment at the Flint Community Schools were forcing the Flint Board of Education to make tough decisions about school facilities. Unfortunately, one result was the closing of eighty-seven-year-old Flint Central High School at the end of the 2008–09 school year. This is one building that needs to be saved. Yes, the building is in need of repair. But it's also at the most ideal location—in the middle of the Flint Cultural Center. The Flint Cultural Center was not there when the high school first opened in September 1923. The location was strictly a happy accident through the years.

Originally the second Flint High School, Central Community High School was built on the Oak Grove Campus facing Crapo Street. The Oak Grove Campus was originally the Oak Grove Hospital or Sanitarium, founded in 1891. It offered patients treatment for nervous and mental diseases and alcohol and drug addiction. It was situated on sixty-one acres of native oak trees, inspiring the name. The land was purchased from Governor Henry Crapo, who had planned to build a mansion on the site. The sanitarium consisted of five buildings interconnected by hallways. The sanitarium decided to dissolve itself in 1919 and sold the campus and buildings to the City of Flint for construction of a high school. The sanitarium closed in 1920.

The original Flint High School at the corner of West Second and Church Streets opened in 1875. In 1915, the building was condemned as a fire trap. It

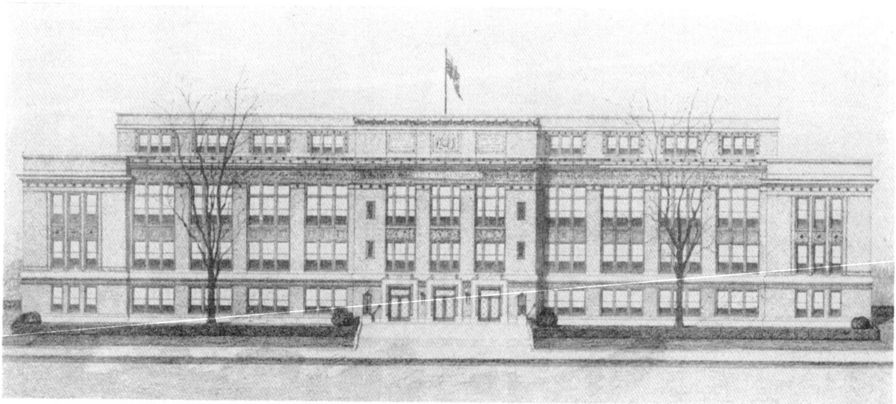

An early drawing of the proposed high school before the Tudor style was adopted, from the 1920 city planning report.

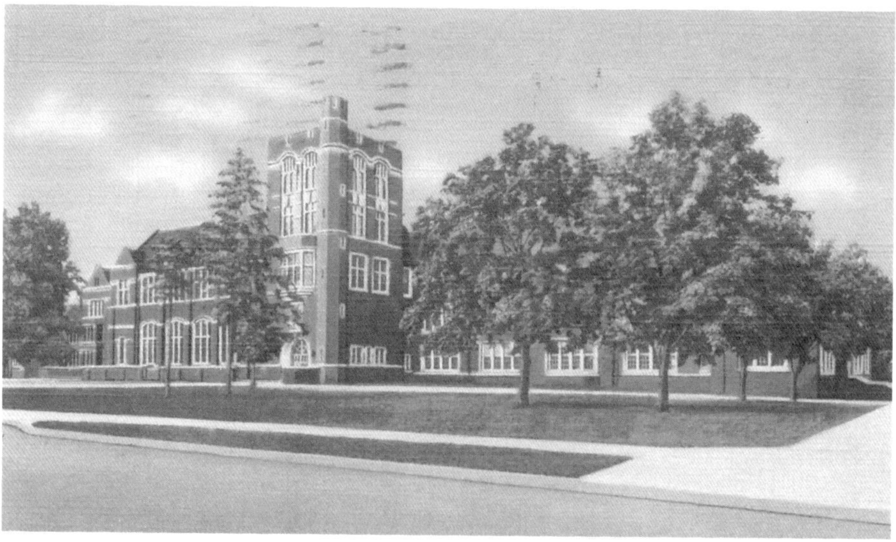

A circa 1941 postcard of Flint Central High School.

continued to be used until a new high school could be built. After the new Flint High School was built, the old high school was converted into South Junior High School, which closed in 1930. It then became a welfare office before the building closed for good in 1936. It was torn down shortly afterward.

Upon taking over the Oak Grove buildings in 1920, the Flint Board of Education made use of them. One building served as the Flint Schools'

Administration Building. Another housed Flint Junior College, now Mott Community College. Flint Junior College's first home was at the new Flint High School, but it outgrew the high school and moved to the Oak Grove Campus in 1931. The buildings also served as an annex for the adjacent high school, which was renamed Central High School in 1928 after the first Northern High was built.

Central High is mostly a three-story, Tudor-style building, but there is also a fourth floor utilizing loft space and the five-story tower. The top floor in the tower can be accessed by a very narrow stairway from the fourth floor. That area is usually closed, but back in the 1970s, I was on the fourth floor, and the door to the fifth-floor stairway was unlocked. I went upstairs to see what was in the tower room. It housed two-way radio transmitting equipment and had a solitary microphone stand in the middle of the room. The walls had acoustical tiles, which indicated that it once housed a radio studio where school programs were recorded for broadcast by the local radio stations before WFBE went on the air.

One notable Oak Grove building was the former Noyes Hall, built in 1895. It originally contained billiard rooms, an assembly hall, a gymnasium, a bowling alley, an electric room and hydrotherapeutic rooms. It was built with funds in part provided by the request of Dr. James F. Noyes, of Detroit, and in part from the revenue of the hospital. Fast-forward to September 30, 1953. The first broadcast from the new FM radio station WFBE went on the air with a dedication program from the new WFBE studio in the renovated Noyes Hall. It was easy to find WFBE on the Oak Grove Campus, as the broadcast tower was adjacent to the studio building.

The 1950s would be the last hurrah for the Oak Grove Campus. In 1955, Flint Junior College moved into the then-new Curtice and Mott Science Buildings on the new nearby campus using land that Charles Stewart Mott donated from his Applewood estate, part of the planned College and Cultural Center. The College and Cultural Center was developed in the 1950s with the Cultural Center buildings surrounding the Oak Grove buildings, with Mott-donated land adjacent to the Oak Grove Campus. Toward the end of the 1950s, the Oak Grove buildings were torn down one by one to make way for a parking lot.

Central High had additions built beginning with the Mechanical Arts & Music (M&M) Building just south of the main building in 1958. Demolition of the last Oak Grove building, the WFBE building, had to wait until the opening of a new two-level addition to Central in 1961 that utilized part of the footprint of a demolished Oak Grove building. The upper level is the new high school cafeteria, and the lower level is the new WFBE studios, offices and transmitting facilities. There was talk in the 1960s about building a new Central High School at the corner of Center Road at Lippincott Boulevard, near the then-new Walli's Restaurant. But in the 1970s, the board of education decided to keep the existing Central High because the building was structurally sound and in a better location. The board decided instead to remodel the high school and build a new field house and swimming pool, which opened in 1975. Enclosed walkways connected the field house with the M&M building and the main high school building.

The Flint Schools' budget problems led to the sale, in 1997, of WFBE, which had become valuable. Unlike most noncommercial radio stations, WFBE operates on a commercial frequency. It was sold for $7 million and signed off as a public radio station on June 30, 1997, airing the same dedication program that had launched the station in 1953. It returned to the air three months later as country music station B95 at a new studio location. The former WFBE studios then housed the Flint Schools' health center. I visited it after a class reunion in 2003 and noticed that no remodeling had taken place. The rooms in the health center were the same as they were when it was the WFBE studios and offices, but without the broadcasting equipment. However, the WFBE transmitter room was still used as the WFBE transmitter room. The window was covered by two window blinds on the inside, but you could see the back-lit modulation meter in the darkened room showing the heavily processed signal pumping up the volume between the window blinds.

Of course, the tall WFBE tower is still in place. The keys to the transmitter room, as well as to the health office to access the transmitter, were held by the Citadel Broadcasting engineers, who maintained the equipment at WFBE and co-owned WTRX. The WFBE/WTRX studios are now on Miller Road across from the Genesee Valley Center. The Flint Board of Education must be grateful for the rental income from WFBE. As a condition of the sale of WFBE, the WFBE owners offer the WFBE/Flint Community Schools Communications Scholarship, which is awarded to selected Flint Community Schools students who study communication arts in college.

When the Flint Schools slated Flint Central High School to close in 2006 or 2007, a movement called the Great Schools Initiative began to influence the

Flint Board of Education to keep open the best schools despite the condition of the school buildings. Being a Flint Central graduate who also worked at WFBE when it was a public radio station in the 1970s, I had a personal interest in keeping Flint Central open. Before it closed, an open house was held on June 12, 2009. The open house was heavily attended, and I was able to look at almost every square inch of the old school. Unfortunately, the fifth-floor tower room was locked, but inside the library, the spiral staircase to the roof of the tower was accessible, giving those who climbed to the top a great view. Several visitors, including myself, had cameras to capture memories of our last look. Remembering WFBE, I also visited the health center, and it was moving out as well. There was a rumor that Flint Powers Catholic High School was interested in buying Flint Central, but Powers's principal denied that they were interested.

In 2010, WFBE moved its transmitting facilities to the co-owned WTRX transmitter building on Bristol Road, near Dort Highway in Burton, utilizing WTRX's tall north tower and leaving Flint Central totally empty. But in the summer of 2010, the Flint Olympian and CANUSA Games office was located and some indoor events were held at Flint Central.

Update: While the school is still closed, there is talk, if money becomes available, to build a new middle/high school on the site of Flint Central and the adjacent old Whittier Middle School to eventually become Flint's only high school. In what became the first sign that my first book was becoming outdated, on October 2010, when the book was first being published, the owners of WFBE radio vacated its former studio location in the lower level of Central. I had mentioned in my previous book that WFBE's owners had built new transmitting facilities in Burton on Bristol Road near Dort Highway at the co-owned WTRX transmitter location, utilizing WTRX's tall north tower mounting WFBE's transmitting antenna on the WTRX tower. After the new transmitting facilities became operational, the owners not only removed the transmitting equipment, but they had also taken down the old WFBE tower, cut it up and put the pieces in a large dumpster. They had neglected to plug up the holes where the transmission line and electrical conduit passed through, making the old transmitter room into a possible habitat for critters. In 2011, WFBE/WTRX's parent company was sold to Cumulus Media, which already owned four Flint radio stations. As a condition of the sale, Cumulus had to dispose of WRSR "The Fox" 103.9

FM, which moved from Cumulus Flint's studio cluster location on Taylor Drive in Mundy Township to the former WFBE/WTRX studio location on Miller Road across from Genesee Valley after WFBE and WTRX were moved to Taylor Drive. A trustee operated WRSR until it was sold to Krol Communications in 2012.

A Tasty Part of Flint History

A deliciously different culinary aspect of Flint history that continues to this day began in 1929. That was when a two-story, Mediterranean-style building with stuccoed walls, arched windows and a tiled roof was built by the Vernor's Ginger Ale Company. It's located downtown at 800 South Saginaw Street and was the company's retail store and sandwich shop, serving the bubbly beverage whose "deliciously different" flavor is aged in oak barrels. A notable feature was an electric sign that depicted in light bulbs a bottle of Vernor's Ginger Ale being poured into a glass. There was also a warehouse on the site where many oak barrels filled with Vernor's Ginger Ale syrup were stored, waiting for the flavor to mellow. Barrels were even stored in underground tunnels between the warehouse and the sandwich shop.

One customer who recalled going there was the late Charles Weinstein. As a child, he bought Vernor's Ginger Ale for his father, Morris Weinstein, who didn't want to be seen patronizing a rival business (he co-owned the M&S Beverage Company). In 1932, sign painters John Gonsowski and Keith Martin, working for General Signs, painted a three-story advertising mural for Vernor's on the north wall of the Sharp Hardware & Implement Company building next door, later known as the Peerless Mattress & Furniture Company building, facing the Vernor's sandwich shop. Mr. Gonsowski was born in Poland and came to Michigan in 1913. He showed his European sensitivities in regard to his painting style. He painted smiling Vernor's gnomes working out of a castle, stacking oak barrels that read, "Flavor mellowed 4 years in wood." Gonsowski painted other Vernor's

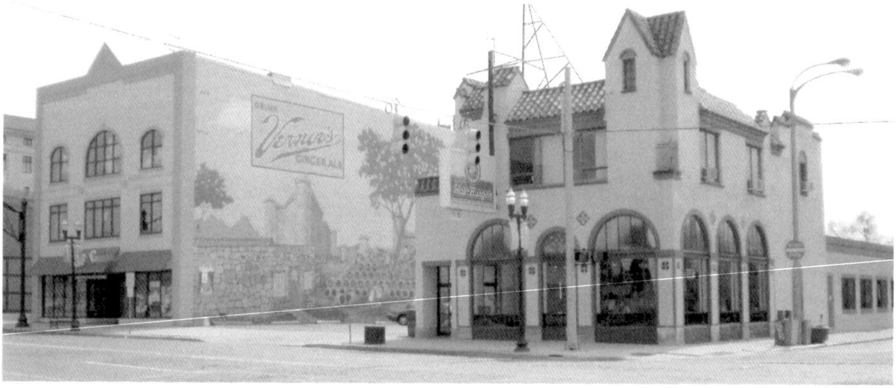

The Halo Burger restaurant and Vernor's mural today.

advertising signs throughout the Flint area. In 1951, Vernor's moved the oak barrels from the site, and James Vernor II sold the sandwich shop to Bill Thomas, the manager of Kewpee Hamburgs, a downtown Flint fixture since 1923. Vernor's took down the pouring bottle sign, and Bill Thomas erected a neon Kewpee sign with the Kewpee doll logo.

The Kewpee Hotel ("Hotel" would later be dropped to avoid confusion among customers, who thought the business offered lodging instead of hamburgers) was founded by Samuel V. Blair, who was nicknamed "Old Man Kewpee," or "the Hamburger King." He was a colorful man who claimed that he originated the flat bun and invented the "deluxe" hamburger. Before arriving in Flint in 1923, he had been an iron molder for thirty years, sold vacuum cleaners and life insurance, studied horticulture and operated orchards. He opened the first Kewpee Hotel at 415 Harrison Street in a wagon-like building. Legend has it that the wagon-like building was buried on the site when it was replaced by a real building, which underwent numerous renovations over the years and was torn down in 1979. For Kewpee Hotel's twentieth anniversary in 1943, Blair gave that day's customers war savings stamps.

William V. "Bill" Thomas came to Flint in 1933 and started working for Blair in 1938. On April 1, 1944, Thomas took over management of the Harrison Street restaurant, leasing the restaurant from Blair, who retired. Characteristically, Blair threw a big retirement party for himself, inviting several friends. Blair died in 1945. The two downtown Flint Kewpees were not the only locations. Why the Kewpee restaurants were called hotels is lost to history.

At its peak, before World War II, there were more than two hundred Kewpee restaurants. The early Kewpees were not franchises, and there was no group association. Each individually owned Kewpee had its own menu with its own style of hamburger. Bill Thomas took full ownership of the Flint Kewpee Hamburgs in 1958, but he couldn't afford the ownership rights to the Kewpee name, which Blair sold to Ed Adams of Toledo. In the early 1960s, Adams wanted to switch from a flat royalty fee to a full franchising arrangement. In 1967, Adams demanded a percentage of the profits from each Kewpee in place of the licensing fees without providing additional support.

Because Bill Thomas did his own advertising and promotion for his Kewpee restaurants, he decided to change the name. On May 12, 1967, the Flint Kewpee restaurants were renamed Bill Thomas's Halo Burger restaurants. Only the name changed. Everything else, including the food, remained the same. Bill Thomas died on Christmas Eve 1973. Today, Bill's son, Terry Thomas, presides over a chain of nine Halo Burger restaurants and take-out stations throughout the Flint area.

After Vernor's sold the sandwich shop to Bill Thomas, the maintenance of the Vernor's mural next door stopped. Over the years, it started to become faded. Bill Thomas wanted to fix it up, but the owner of Peerless Mattress resisted having the mural maintained. It wasn't until the Greater Flint Arts Council's Urban Walls Committee, which commissioned murals in downtown Flint, stepped in wanting to restore the Vernor's mural that Peerless Mattress finally agreed. Halo Burger donated $27,000 for the restoration of the mural in 1979, including two additions to the mural in place of blank wall space. The restoration and additions were done by Donna Devantier and Michael Perry of Eller Outdoor Advertising. Original artist John Gonsowski was on hand during the restoration.

On the large mural addition to the right of the original mural, a small extension to the castle, an open field and houses in the background were added. As a tribute to Halo Burger, a cow with a halo over its head was painted. Halo Burger's mascot is an angelic cow. After the mural was completed, the mural was coated with a sealant to protect it.

When Vernor's built the sandwich shop, it included a small building, or guardhouse, and gates for the delivery trucks to go through. The small building was at one time Pete's Diner, run by Peter Parascos. Through the years, it also housed May's Lunch, Tom's Lunch and Thomas's Pantry Shoppe. It finally became storage before it was torn down to aid in the mural restoration and provide additional parking for Halo Burger. The small mural addition that occupies the spot where the small building stood features a painted guardhouse for the castle with a winking gnome looking through the window.

In 1995, the Peerless Mattress building was gutted in an arson fire that forced Peerless to move to the suburbs. The Vernor's mural was undamaged in the fire, but the building the mural was painted on was threatened. Fundraising to buy the building and fix it up was successful, saving it from demolition, and the Greater Flint Arts Council moved in to the former Peerless Mattress building. In 2001, the mural received a second restoration. Steve Davidek and Stephen Heddy (both of whom worked on a mural restoration at the Genesee County Court House) worked on the second restoration, which was funded by the Ruth Mott Foundation. The owner of Vernors in 1979 did not help with the first restoration, but Dr Pepper/Seven Up, Inc., which took over Vernors in 1994, contributed funds to help save the Peerless building.

Over the years, the Halo Burger location that was formerly Vernor's and Kewpee had additions built that are faithful to the building's original design. The Flint Kewpee locations pioneered drive-thru take-out windows and burgers with olives. When the original Kewpee/Halo Burger was torn down in 1979 to make room for parking for the new University of Michigan–Flint downtown campus, the staff moved to a new Halo Burger location on Court Street, near Center Road, serving Flint's east side. There are only five Kewpee locations left: one Michigan location in Lansing; one in Racine, Wisconsin; and three at Kewpee's current home base of Lima, Ohio. Vernors lost the apostrophe in its name when the company went public following the death of James Vernor III in 1957 at age thirty-nine; the company needed additional capital. The Vernor family reluctantly sold the ginger ale company in 1966 because of estate tax problems dating back to the death of James Vernor II in 1954.

Of course, you can still order a Vernors at Halo Burger, which offers a Boston Cooler made with Vernors and vanilla ice cream. It is a refreshing treat during the summer months. The old Kewpee slogan is: "Hamburg, pickle on top! Makes your heart go flippity flop!" Halo Burger's slogan is: "Seven days without a Halo Burger makes one weak."

Thanks to Greg Fiedler of the Greater Flint Arts Council, Terry Thomas at Bill Thomas's Halo Burger and Karen Kassel, the great-granddaughter of original Vernor's mural painter John Gonsowski.

Update: In 2010, the Thomas family sold the Halo Burger chain to local Subway franchisee Dortch Enterprises. In 2016, the chain was sold again to a Michigan group, forming Halo Country LLC as the parent company to Halo Burger, which changed the Halo Burger logo.

First Street Lofts

Redevelopment of urban areas often develops into a "chicken and egg" issue, as in: "Which comes first, the chicken or the egg?" This scenario locally involves trying to keep people in downtown Flint after 5:00 p.m., a task that, in recent years, has become increasingly challenging. Developing downtown housing is one way to keep people downtown after 5:00 p.m. Previous attempts have produced spotty results.

But the restoration and redevelopment of downtown Flint's Republic Bank Building changed all that. This time, the redevelopment was in the heart of downtown instead of on the outskirts, as in the case of Carriage Town. The Republic Bank Building at 460 South Saginaw Street was an appropriately historical building for restoration and conversion of the upper floors to the First Street Lofts apartments.

The Republic Bank Building was known by different names over the years. It was built in 1924 as the First National Bank Building. An addition to the rear of the building was constructed in 1928, increasing the building's depth from 100 to 150 feet. This Neoclassical building was clad in white terra cotta surrounding the Palladian, or arched, steel windows and was inspired by the City Beautiful movement, which followed the White City World's Columbian Exposition in Chicago in 1893.

The bank first opened in 1858 as the Exchange Bank and became First National Bank in 1865. It was renamed the National Bank of Flint

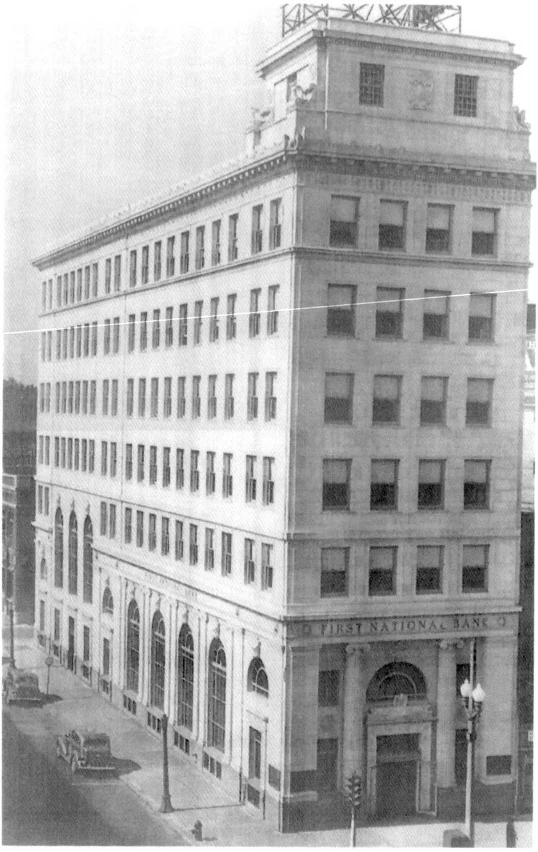

A vintage photo of the First National Bank Building, now First Street Lofts. *Courtesy of Freeman Greer.*

in 1905 and merged with the Genesee County Savings Bank in 1916. This left Flint without a nationally chartered bank, so all of the Flint banks were chartered by the State of Michigan. Genesee Bank spun off of the acquired bank in 1918 and received a new national bank charter, becoming First National Bank again. It had occupied its location at 326 South Saginaw Street, at Kearsley Street, since 1875 and had outgrown that location, leading to the opening of the new office on March 20, 1924. An early 1920s construction photo indicated that it was built by "H.L. Vander Horst, General Contractor, J. Sorenseen, Architect, Kalamazoo, Grand Rapids."

The First National Bank did not survive the Great Depression, closing permanently during the 1933 Bank Holiday. The impounded deposits of that bank and the closed Union Industrial Bank were freed by the formation of a new bank, chartered in December 1933, called the National Bank of Flint and located at the former Union Industrial Bank location in the Union Industrial (now Mott Foundation) Building at the opposite corner of Saginaw and First Streets. The president of that bank was Robert T. Longway. That bank was sold in 1942 to Lansing-based Michigan National Bank, which is now Bank of America's local operations.

The First National Building was sold in 1935 to William S. Ballenger from the closed bank's receiver for $310,000. In 1937, the former First National Bank space became the home of Morrison's women's clothing store. The building was renamed the National Building. In remodeling the former bank space, three of the Palladian windows, including the front window over the door, were removed to make room for Morrison's neon signs designed with 1920s-style, "ultramodern" lettering. The cornice on the roof was also removed.

In 1966, the National Building was sold by the Flint Junior College Ballenger Trust to the First Federal Savings & Loan Association of Flint. The trust was established after Ballenger's death in 1951. First Federal was founded in 1934 and had outgrown its main office on West Kearsley Street. After two years of planning and construction of their new location, Morrison's moved, in 1968, to make room for the savings and loan, and the building became home to a financial institution again. The new main office of First Federal Savings opened in 1969 after a year of renovation, which unfortunately involved modernizing the exterior, the trend in renovating old buildings at that time. The first- and second-floor façades facing Saginaw and First were changed to a modern appearance using red granite and white marble. The back façade facing Buckham Alley was not changed, so there was still one Palladian window. The building was renamed the First Federal Building.

In May 1977, First Federal officials decided to close its building to renters and gave its tenants notice to move out by January 1, 1978. The S&L lost $47,000 in 1976 keeping the building open to renters. While the office building was 60 percent occupied in 1977, the building showed no profit for quite a long time. First Federal occupied the basement and the first and second floors. It had plans to expand to the third floor. The fourth through seventh floors were mothballed until such time as it would be economically feasible to use them again.

The sale of First Federal Savings of Flint to Detroit & Northern Savings & Loan Association meant another name change in 1982, this time to the

Detroit & Northern, or D&N, Building. D&N Savings was reorganized into D&N Bank, a Federal Savings Bank, in 1990. D&N itself was sold and consolidated in 1999 into Republic Bank, a state-chartered bank founded in Flint in 1985.

The building was declared a historic landmark by the State of Michigan in 1980 and was given local historic designation by the Flint Historical District Commission in 1984. A Michigan historical marker is next to the front entrance.

In 2005, after a long gestation period, construction began on the First Street Lofts. The top five floors of former office space were converted to loft apartments with hardwood floors, granite counter tops and stainless-steel appliances. The exterior was restored to how it looked back in 1927. Because terra cotta building material is no longer in production, castings made out of concrete and fiberglass approved for restoration projects are being used; $1.6 million of the $6 million investment has been allocated for the exterior restoration. The building was listed on the National Register of Historic Places. Funding and support came from a variety of sources, including the C.S. Mott Foundation, the Ruth Mott Foundation, the Bishop Trust, the Michigan Historic Preservation Office, the National Parks Service, Uptown Developments, LLC, Uptown Reinvestment Corporation, the City of Flint, Genesee County and the Community Foundation of Greater Flint.

Sixteen one-bedroom and two-bedroom apartments were developed, two on the third floor, four on the fourth and fifth floors and three on the sixth and seventh floors. The best thing about this project is that Uptown Developments fielded calls daily during construction from those interested in leasing apartments, and at least six leases were signed before the project was completed in 2006. The following year, First Street Lofts received the Governor's Award for Historic Preservation.

Republic Bank continued to occupy the first and second floors, but when it merged with Citizens Bank, the redundant bank closed. This successful development helped spur further redevelopment of downtown properties, including the renovated Rowe Building, Community Foundation Building and the newly constructed Wade Trim Building.

Thanks to architect Freeman Greer of GAV & Associates Inc., Ridgway White and Scott Whipple of Uptown Developments, LLC, and former Republic Bank director Gary Hurand.

Goodbye, WFDF

In 2005, an institution that was a part of the Flint area for eighty-three years broadened its reach and shifted its target audience toward Detroit. Flint's first radio station, WFDF, now better known as Radio Disney broadcasting on the AM dial at 910 kHz, moved its transmitting facilities from its longtime Burton location at the corner of Bristol and Howe to new, larger transmitting facilities near Carleton in Monroe County, southwest of Detroit. The station is now licensed to the Detroit suburb of Farmington Hills.

WFDF's founder was Frank D. Fallain. Fallain was born in Fort Wayne, Indiana, on January 13, 1890, and came to Flint from Wisconsin in 1905. His interest in wireless radio began as a hobby in 1909. From 1912 to 1915, he attended the Marconi School at Columbia University. He freelanced and studied in Europe before returning to Flint to open Flint's first radio station.

The station was licensed by the U.S. Department of Commerce on May 25, 1922, with the call letters WEAA at 1070 kHz. The call letters were changed, using Fallain's initials, to WFDF in 1925. On the first day of broadcasting, July 10, 1922, the broadcast included talk and musical selections by local artists. The signal was heard as far away as Long Island, New York. The station's first home was in the Walsh Building at 310 North Saginaw Street. During the summer, large crowds would gather on the Saginaw Street Bridge to listen to concerts amplified from one of the windows of the building.

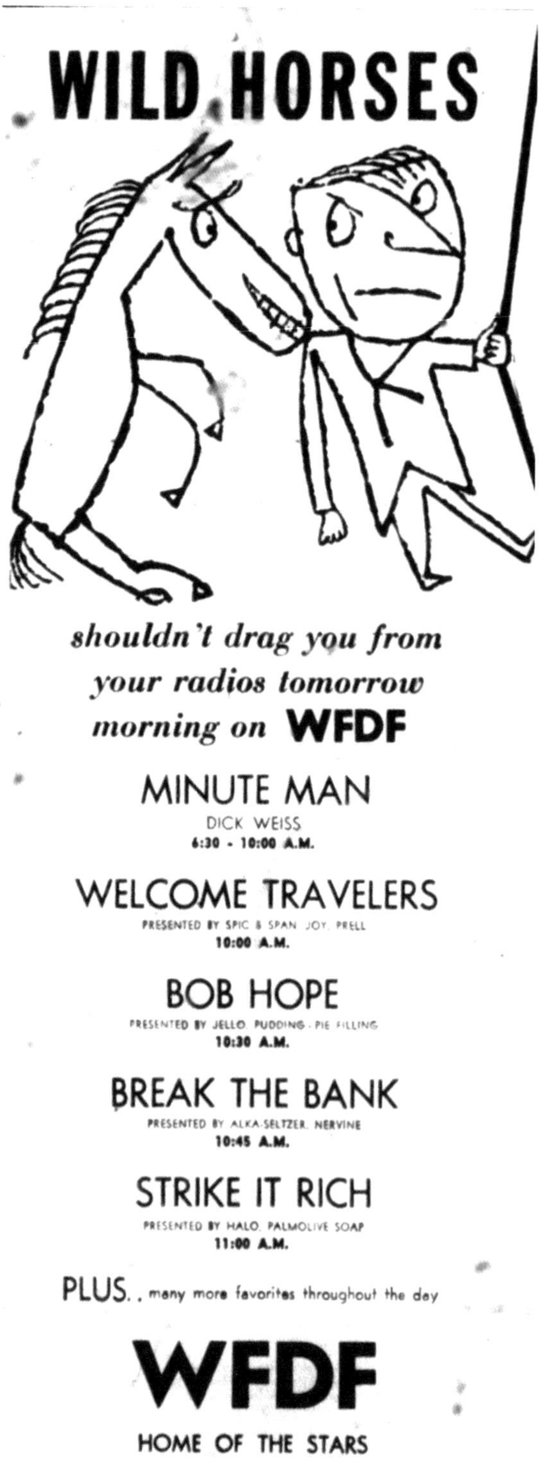

A 1954 vintage WFDF ad.

Fallain also operated the station for a short time from the Flint Police Station, where his small staff helped police by broadcasting descriptions of stolen cars and wanted outlaws, as well as airing public service announcements. The station's first remote broadcast in 1925 originated from Lakeside Park along Thread Lake, near Peer Avenue, where Billy Mills and his orchestra performed. By that time, the station had moved to 1280 kHz on the dial; it then moved to 860 kHz the following year. It changed frequencies again by 1928 to 1100 kHz and then to 1310 kHz by 1930. In 1940, WFDF increased its power to one thousand watts and settled on its present frequency, 910 kHz.

The station also pioneered in other fields, broadcasting election returns, a Flint mayor's inaugural address and excerpts of city commission meetings, which were later broadcast live. In 1928, WFDF moved to new studios and offices on the sixteenth floor of the Union Industrial Bank (now Mott Foundation) Building, where it was used to present programs by the Flint Community Music Association and the St. Cecilia Society. The two towers that supported a long wire antenna are still in place.

Fallain sold WFDF in 1933 to the Loeb brothers but continued as president and technical director until he retired in 1952. Frank D. Fallain died on November 3, 1968, at McLaren General Hospital at age seventy-eight. He was survived by his wife, Dorothy Fallain.

WFDF was part of radio's golden age in the pre-television era, airing early radio programs such as *The Lone Ranger* and other network shows from the Michigan Radio Network and the NBC Blue Network, which would become the ABC Radio Network after NBC was forced to divest itself of one of its two networks (the Red and the Blue).

The station was sold in 1948 to the Trebit Corp., which tried unsuccessfully in the 1950s to build a TV station on channel 12, losing to Goodwill Stations, Inc., the owner of WJR, which put WJRT on the air. WFDF also abandoned plans in the early 1950s to start an FM station. The station moved to larger quarters in 1952 at the corner of First Avenue and Garland, where the TV station would have been located had Trebit won the rights to channel 12.

As TV took over as the prime source of entertainment, WFDF developed into a prime source for news and information featuring middle-of-the-road music. The morning man for decades was Dan Hunter, who joined WFDF in 1948. Pete Sark was WFDF's sports director. Betty Clarke presented homemaking tips on her call-in show, *Party Line*. In 1953, WFDF switched its network affiliation from ABC to NBC and aired NBC's now legendary *Monitor* radio shows on weekends. In 1956, WFDF was sold to the Crowell-Collier Publishing Company.

In 1957, WFDF received authorization from the Federal Communications Commission to increase its transmitting power to five thousand watts daytime and one thousand watts nighttime, giving WFDF a strong signal north, covering the tri-cities and beyond. WFDF Flint Corp., a partnership of Howard Mack and Dan Cowin, became owner of the station in 1961, with Mack becoming sole owner in 1964. Mack died in 1967, and his widow, Fanne, became WFDF's owner.

Veteran radio newsman Les Root joined WFDF from WTRX in 1970. Another noted reporter at WFDF was David Leyton, who was later elected Genesee County prosecutor.

In 1971, WFDF was persuaded to go after younger listeners by airing more rock music. This alienated older listeners, until the station came up with a more adult contemporary mix of music. In 1976, WFDF switched its network affiliation from NBC Radio to CBS Radio and, in 1978, moved to state-of-the-art studios and offices in the Phoenix Building. It began broadcasting twenty-four hours a day. This carried the station through until the 1980s, when it started losing listeners to FM radio. Betty Clarke (real name Betty Monas) retired in 1983 and now lives in Surprise, Arizona, thirty-five miles from Phoenix.

The year 1985 marked the beginning of the end for WFDF as Fanne Mack Pelavin sold the station for $750,000 to the owner of WDZZ (FM), Vernon Merritt Jr. Merritt then fired eleven WFDF staff members while keeping Dan Hunter and Les Root. Except for Dan Hunter, the programming was satellite fed. WDZZ moved some of its operations to the Phoenix Building. Dan Hunter was happy when the station came up with an adult standards format featuring the big band music he loved; he retired in 1988. Dan Hunter died in 1995. He was succeeded by veteran broadcast personality Ed Berryman. Also in 1988, Merritt sold WFDF and WDZZ to Erie Coast Communications, Inc., for $6.5 million, and WFDF moved to 1401 South Saginaw Street to save rent money. The following year, WFDF joined WDZZ, sharing studios and offices at Genesee Towers. In 1990, both stations were sold to McVay Broadcasting for more than $7 million.

McVay sold both stations in 1994 to Connoisseur Communications. The following year, the new owners changed WFDF's format from adult standards to news/talk. But the transition to the new format was less than graceful. On October 30, 1995, Ed Berryman began his 5:00 a.m. to 10:00 a.m. morning shift and was given an unfamiliar playlist of pop hits from the 1960s and '70s and ordered to air them. Berryman was unable to contact the station's general manager about the changes during his shift. So, at the end of his shift at 10:00 a.m., the frustrated Berryman announced on the air that he quit. The forty-nine-year veteran of Flint radio deserved better treatment by WFDF management. Berryman moved over to WFBE to host a similar big band/nostalgia show until he retired.

In 1997, Connoisseur added four more radio stations to its Flint station cluster by buying WWCK-AM-FM, WOAP (AM, later sold) and WAHV (FM, now WRSR) from Majac of Michigan. By 1999, Connoisseur had consolidated all the stations' studios and offices to the Flint Radio Center on Taylor Drive, off Hill Road in Mundy Township. Cumulus Media bought the thirty-five-station Connoisseur Communications group, including the Flint cluster of stations, in 2000. In 2002, Cumulus received an offer it couldn't refuse. ABC, Inc., waved $3 million at Cumulus, and Cumulus sold WFDF to ABC, a unit of Disney. ABC's plans were to make WFDF the southeast Michigan station for Radio Disney. On August 15, 2002, WFDF changed formats from news/talk to the satellite-fed Radio Disney pop music format aimed at nine- to twelve-year-olds and their moms.

The following year, ABC applied to the FCC for a construction permit to increase the station's daytime power to fifty thousand watts with the transmitter located in Monroe County. To allow that to happen, ABC bought an AM station in Fremont, Ohio, near Toledo, that operated at 900 kHz and shut it down in 2004. Also in 2004, ABC applied for nighttime power of nineteen thousand watts from the proposed Monroe County site and also applied to change the city of license to Farmington Hills. The new transmitting facilities were completed and operational in 2005. During the testing phase, the WFDF signal was nonexistent in Flint, as the station was operating at reduced power from the new location. While the station was still licensed to Flint, Radio Disney was legally bound to maintain offices in the Flint area. The office was located in the Grand Mall in Grand Blanc. The city of license was changed to Farmington Hills in February 2006. The towers of the former transmitting location at the corner of Bristol and

Howe, in use since 1940, were taken down in April 2006. Around that time, the local offices were moved to the Detroit suburb of Southfield.

The station is currently licensed to Radio Disney Group, LLC. It's sad that a pioneering radio station with a rich history has literally become a Mickey Mouse operation.

Thanks to Marvin Levey and Betty Monas.

Update: In 2014, Radio Disney changed its focus and sold nearly all its terrestrial radio stations, including WFDF. WFDF was sold to the Word Network, led by Kevin Adell, which took over the station in 2015, still based in the Detroit suburb of Southfield. Under Adell, WFDF initially aired a religious format before switching over to an urban talk format in 2016 and calling itself the 910 AM Superstation.

Downtown Flint's Coney Island Restaurants

There is a reason the Coney Island hot dog got its name. The hot dog was invented at Coney Island in New York by Charles Feltman in 1867 as a new kind of hot fast food he could easily sell from a push cart. He put a Vienna sausage in a sliced roll and called it a "Coney Island Red Hot." Some people, unsure of its ingredients, called it a "hot dog." Feltman's hot dog sold so well that he opened a restaurant at Coney Island. One employee at Feltman's was Nathan Handwerker, who began working there in 1915 and saved enough money to start his own hot dog business in 1916. This was the start of Nathan's Famous, whose flagship restaurant is a Coney Island landmark. Nathan's Famous had a location on Linden Road in Flint at the Lincor Plaza, inside Kenny Rogers Roasters, which was acquired by Nathan's in 1999. But its hot dogs could not successfully compete with Flint's variation of the Coney Island hot dog, and the local Nathan's/Kenny Rogers franchise closed up shop in 2003.

The main ingredient of Flint's version of the Coney Island hot dog is the sausage itself, which is traditionally a Koegel's Vienna made with natural casings. That is what gives the Flint Coney its snap when you bite into it. Koegel makes a special Coney version of Viennas that is only available wholesale to restaurants. This variety of Vienna sausage is made to be held on a grill for an extended period of time. So you can only get a Flint Coney Island at a restaurant that serves them.

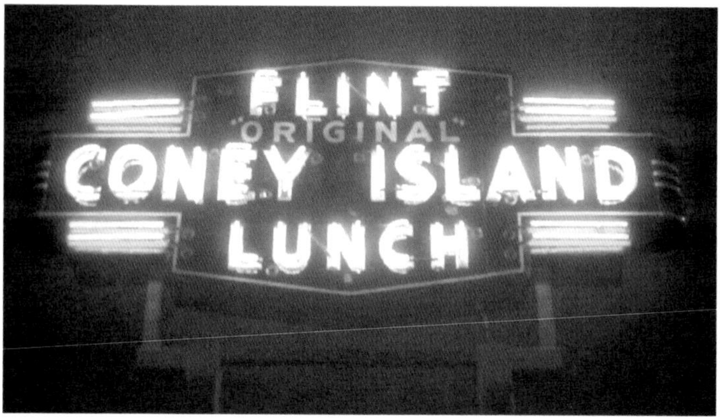

A restored "Flint Original Coney Island" neon sign, now at Tom Z's Flint Original Coney Island.

Albert Koegel was a German who learned the sausage making business as an apprentice in Germany. He then immigrated to the United States to start a new life. A salesman for Armour Foods suggested that Koegel move to Flint, as he stood a good chance for success in the growing city. Koegel moved to Flint and established Koegel Meats in 1916. By the mid-1930s, he had built the business up enough to start his own manufacturing operation to produce his own meat products. The plant was downtown where the University of Michigan–Flint is now located. It moved to a larger plant at its present location on Bristol Road near Bishop Airport in 1972.

Flint's version of the Coney Island is noted for its dry meat sauce, compared to the Detroit variety, which is more watery. The original Flint-style sauce is said to contain byproducts such as beef heart and kidney. The variety of spices varied in the secret recipes from one restaurant to another. The Flint Coney Island restaurants developed with the arrival of Greek and Macedonian immigrants in the 1910s and 1920s. They came to Flint seeking opportunities in the growing city. For decades, Coney Island restaurants were in operation downtown, just south of the Flint River, until they were torn down for urban renewal in the 1970s.

The first restaurant to open was Flint Coney Island (aka Flint Original Coney Island) in about 1925. It was founded by Steve George, George Brown and Sam Brown. It was located at 202 (later 208) South Saginaw Street. Competition began four years later, when George Pappadakis, George J. Pappadakis and Michael Pappas opened New System Coney Island next door, at 200½ (later 208, then 200) South Saginaw Street. George Brown joined with Gus Thomas to open U.S. Coney Island at 110 South Saginaw

Street about 1935. About 1938, two more Coney Island restaurants opened in the same downtown area. Famous Coney Island was opened by George J. Poulos at 116 South Saginaw Street, and Tasty Coney Island was opened by Gust. A. Yeotis and Harry A. Yeotis at 201 South Saginaw. In 1945, the Hot Puppy Coney Island, owned by Gus Thomas and Robert L. Kerner, replaced New System Coney Island at 200 South Saginaw. It only lasted a year before it was acquired and became U.S. Coney Island #2, run by Louis P. Angelefsky, Mike D. Stublensky and William Stevens. By that time, U.S. Coney Island #1 was operated by Stevens and Angelefsky. Angelefsky helped run #2 when U.S. #1 took it over. By 1953, Mike D. Stublensky had bought U.S. Coney Island #2 and renamed it Mike's Coney Island. It changed hands again by 1964, when Nick Markovich renamed it Nick's Coney Island. It later became Mike's Coney Island again in 1966, run by Mike Sablinski.

The first of the downtown Coney Island restaurants near the Flint River to close was Tasty Coney Island in 1965. Gus A. Yeotis ran it in its final years. Mike's Coney Island closed in 1971; it was run by Richard Lemmon and Kenneth Pell. U.S. Coney Island, run by Nicholas and George Sfetkidis, was forced to close in 1973 to make way for Riverbank Park. Flint Original Coney Island, the first downtown Coney restaurant, was the last one to close when Simeon Panoff and Boris R. Christoff closed it for the last time in 1978 to make way for the Hyatt Regency Hotel (now the Riverfront Residence Hall). But Coney lovers still had the neighborhood Coney Island restaurants, including longtime east side landmark Angelo's at the corner of Davison Road and Franklin Avenue leading the list of fourteen Coney restaurants serving Flint's neighborhoods that year. I shouldn't forget Starlite Coney Island on the Burton side of Center Road.

With the growth of Flint's suburbs, Coney restaurants opened to serve suburbia. Examples include Gillie's, Mt. Morris and Sam's Coney Islands in Mt. Morris and Mega Coney Island in Fenton. Downtown Flint has Tom Z's Flint Original Coney Island, at 401 West Court Street, which features the restored Flint Original Coney Island neon sign from its original downtown location.

The Flint variety of the Coney Island hot dog is indeed a unique and flavorful part of Flint's history that continues to be enjoyed. You can enjoy it, too, with the following easy recipe:

FLINT-STYLE CONEY ISLAND SAUCE

1 tablespoon butter
1 tablespoon margarine
1 ½ pounds lean ground beef
2 medium onions, minced
1 clove garlic, minced
3 tablespoons chili powder
1 tablespoon prepared mustard
1 6 oz. can tomato paste
1 6 oz. can water
Salt and pepper to taste
4 or 5 cheap skinless hot dogs

Do not brown beef before using. Combine all ingredients, except hot dogs, and simmer until thick. Grind the hot dogs (or chop in a food processor), stir into mixture and cook 15 minutes longer. If the sauce is a little thin, you can add crumbled soda crackers. It can be stored in the refrigerator or freezer. Always serve with Koegel's Viennas.

If you don't have time to make your own Coney sauce, you can buy a box of Gracie's Famous Original Coney Island Sauce, made by Gracie's Kitchen, Inc., and available at some local supermarkets in the hot dog section.

Chronology based on information found in city directory listings. Thanks to Koegel Meats.

The Capitol Theatre

A Downtown Flint Jewel

Probably the most beautiful building in downtown Flint is the Capitol Theatre building designed by world-renowned theater architect John Eberson (1875–1955). Eberson pioneered the atmospheric theater design in which the theater simulated an outdoor patio indoors, complete with stars (light bulbs), clouds (projected by "cloud machines") and lighting that depicted a sunset to start the show and a sunrise to end the show. The Capitol is a classic Eberson atmospheric theater with an Italian renaissance motif to bring, as the opening night program stated, "a touch of Italy transferred in its seductive charms to the City of Flint." Sitting in the Capitol Theatre, it was as if you were on the patio of an old Italian garden under a Mediterranean night sky.

The theater was first conceived by J. Bradford Pengelly, who bought the property where the Capitol sits today in 1923. It had previously been the site of the Bachtel "ten-cent sheds" (where you could leave your horse all day for a dime). By 1923, automobiles had replaced horses on downtown Flint streets. Pengelly's group (which also included Arthur M. Davison, John L. Pierce and Edwin W. Atwood) got together with theater chain owner Walter S. Butterfield, and together they formed the Flint Capitol Building Company in March 1924. The company began building the three-story structure housing a theater, arcade, stores, offices and a basement bowling alley in April 1927. Legal hassles involving getting clear title to the property had delayed construction until that time. The theater opened on Thursday,

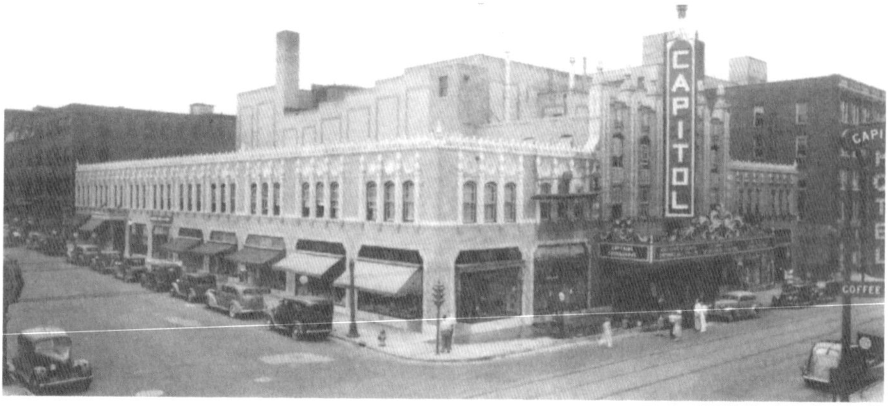

A vintage exterior photo of the Capitol Theatre.

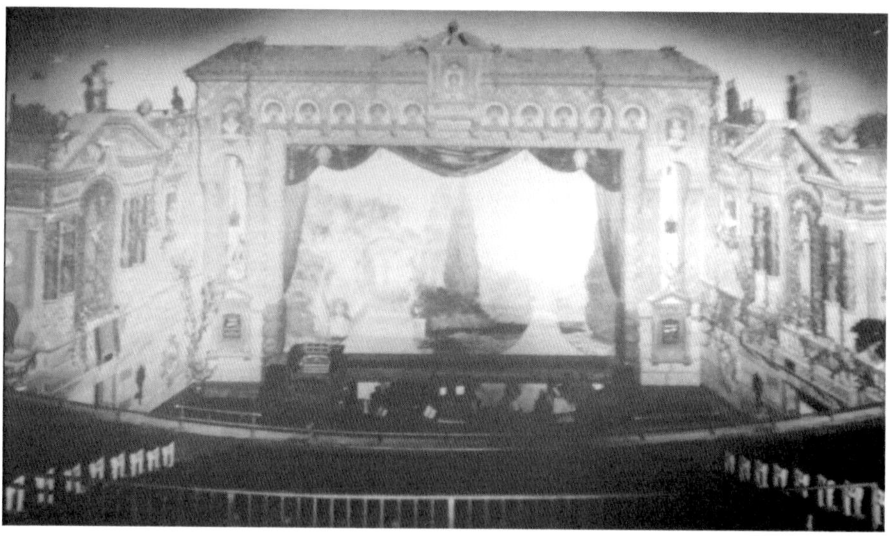

A vintage interior photo before the Capitol Theatre was remodeled in 1957.

January 19, 1928. W.S. Butterfield Theatres operated the theater from day one until it first closed in 1976. Butterfield Theatres remodeled the theater in 1957 by modernizing the lobby, removing much of the inside ornamentation and repainting the theater interior (which was cream in color) battleship gray. An addition to the third story (with less ornamentation compared to the rest of the façade) was also built.

In 1977, local grocer George Farah bought the Capitol Theatre building from the Windiate-Pierce-Davison Company, which ran the Flint Capitol Building Company, and he, along with at least three other people who leased the theater from Farah over the years, tried unsuccessfully to run the theater. Former city councilman Woody Etherly briefly owned the theater, but he was not successful, so Farah repossessed the building. It was last used in the 1990s for punk rock shows in the theater, the lobby and the former bowling alley space in the basement, which was called the "Fallout Shelter." A bar was also in business in the lobby, appropriately called The Lobby. The Farah family had been doing archaeological demolition of the remodeled space to reveal hidden plaster details. But a full restoration would cost between $20 and $25 million. The Farah family does not have the money, so they have been working on fixing the theater in phases. They received approval in March 2004 from the Flint Historic District Commission to make necessary repairs and received a matching grant of $50,000 from the Ruth Mott Foundation to make exterior repairs budgeted at $100,000.

Repairs began in late August 2004 with the removal and replacement of water-damaged brick from the east exterior wall of the auditorium. Work then shifted to the west wall of the theater, along Brush Alley, replacing most of the water-damaged brick on that wall. The repaired wall along Brush Alley was spot painted. The most notable repairs were of the vertical sign, which is original to the theater, and the canopy over the arcade and office building entrance along Harrison Street, also original to the building. Over several months, the Harrison Street canopy was repaired so that it now looks similar to the way it looked originally, with additional ornamentation added on top of the canopy to enhance its appearance at great expense. The vertical sign had its neon removed and was power washed before it was repainted. Rust damage on the sign was patched over in the process. There was enough money in the budget to install new neon and electrically restore the sign so that when the sign is operational, the two layers of neon will alternately flash CAPITOL and THEATRE like they did many years ago.

These repairs have used up the $100,000 budget. It's estimated that it would take another $500,000 to completely restore the façade. This would include replacing damaged stonework, replicating missing trim on the vertical sign (blown off in a storm several years ago), replacing the large ornament that originally topped the vertical sign (removed in the 1950s), installing a new canopy marquee similar to the original one (the smaller Harrison Street canopy is similar underneath) and restoring the theater entrance. These repairs, as well as restoring the theater itself, may require a rich benefactor.

Let's hope the improvements underway in downtown Flint will make it possible to fully restore the Capitol Theatre, an irreplaceable and precious resource. There are only a dozen or so Eberson-designed atmospheric theaters left standing in the United States out of about 130 built.

Thanks to Troy Farah.

Update: While under private ownership, the Farah family was able to do a partial restoration of the Capitol Theatre's lobby area, with work underway to restore more of the theater building. But under private ownership, money was not available for a full restoration. So the Farah family sold the Capitol Theatre in 2015 to a nonprofit unit of Uptown Reinvestment Corp. The new owner is the Friends of the Capitol Theatre, which immediately announced restoration plans originally estimated to cost $21 million. Restoration work began in 2016. The group is partnering with the Flint Cultural Center Corporation and the Whiting Auditorium, which will manage the Capitol Theatre, including programming and marketing, with a planned opening date in late 2017. The marquee and blade sign were replicated by Signs by Crannie with aluminum using LED light bulbs and electronic attraction boards, with the center board still using hanging letters. The plain-looking third-story addition was torn down, the offices and storefronts rehabilitated and the theater restored inside and out to the way it looked in 1928, with state-of-the-art stage equipment along with a digital projector and a new screen to show movies. Part of the arcade is incorporated into the lobby with first-floor restrooms, an additional elevator and a relocated refreshment stand. The theater, meeting modern building codes, has a reduced seating capacity with 1,500 brand-new retro-style seats. Plans are to donate the old signs to the Sloan Museum.

Community Schools

A Flint Invention

In 1935, during the Great Depression, Flint was going through a major economic downturn with thousands of people out of work. The young people in the city had little to do after school. Some of them were getting into trouble. At that time, the local schools were locked up after school ended for the day. But a physical education instructor with the Flint Schools named Frank Manley had an idea.

Manley expressed his concerns to a meeting of the local Rotary Club. He complained that the school system, as it was operated, was ill equipped to support the social needs of the community. Manley proposed opening school buildings on evenings and weekends, as well as during the summer, as a means of reducing what was then called juvenile delinquency.

Fortunately, Manley had a like-minded friend who had similar concerns but also had the money to carry out Manley's ideas. Charles Stewart Mott was at the Rotary Club meeting and was impressed with Manley's leadership abilities. After a series of tennis matches and discussions at Mott's Applewood estate, Manley and Mott pitched the idea to members of the Flint Board of Education. They liked the idea, so Mott donated $6,000 to the Flint Schools to support supervised afterschool and Saturday activities for children and adults.

It was first called the Mott Program and began with five schools. The program was so successful that First Lady Eleanor Roosevelt visited Flint

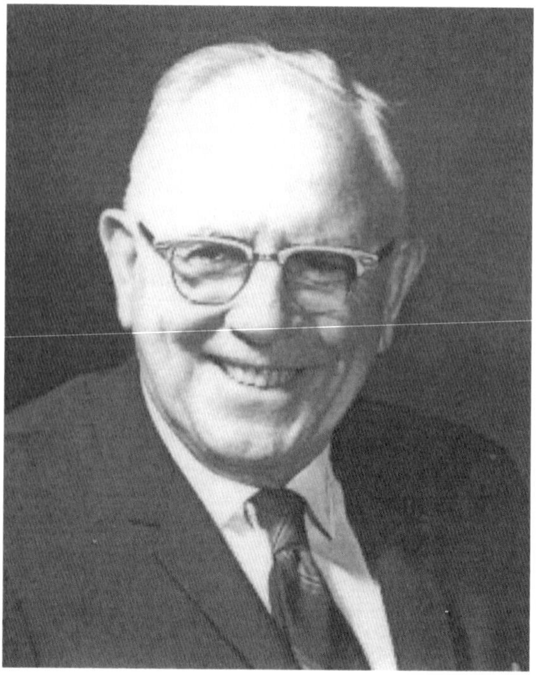

Frank Manley.

in 1936 to see the school activities for herself. Officials from other school districts around the country and internationally visited Flint to get ideas for their own afterschool and summer programs. Because other school districts started hiring away Flint school officials to launch their own programs, a need arose for training programs. In 1964, the Mott Foundation launched the Mott Intern Program based at the Mott Leadership Center. The center became the National Center for Community Education (NCCE) in the early 1970s, located in Flint at the Crawford House at 1017 Avon Street. In 1974, President Gerald Ford signed the Community School and Comprehensive Community Education Act, appropriating $3 million annually for community education programs and establishing a federal Office of Community Education.

Locally, the Mott Program eventually expanded into every Flint school, becoming Community Schools. Every school had a community school director who ran the afterschool and summer programs. As the Flint Board of Education built new schools after World War II to handle the baby boom, it included amenities like large gymnasiums where many of the community school programs were held. Most of the older schools in the Flint system had

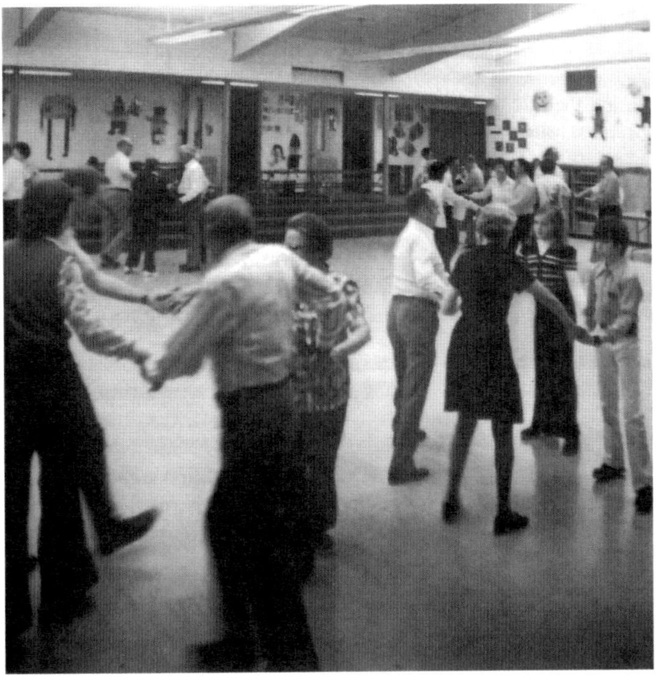

Square dancing for all ages.

additions built that included large gyms. These schools became community centers in their neighborhoods.

In 2006, the Flint Community Schools operated two community education programs aimed at children. One was the 21st Century Community Learning Centers (21st CCLC), an NCCE-originated program in which the Flint Schools actively take part today. Five elementary schools—Bunche, Brownell, Civic Park, Stewart and Washington—are the learning center locations. The purpose of the initiative is to support and fortify students' learning through coordinated and integrated extended learning opportunities. The Flint Project targeted these schools, whose students have demonstrated a need for academic support services, and they were transformed into community learning centers. The project provided an opportunity for students and their families to continue to learn new skills and discover new abilities after the end of the school day. In the summer of 2006, the five schools in the program had a summer program running from July 10 to August 3. Students explored other cultures in the morning as they embarked on a "voyage" that took them to Jamaica, Germany, Egypt and Japan. The afternoon was spent doing a host of recreational and social development activities.

The other program at the Flint Community Schools that began in 2006 was the Bridges to the Future (BTF), a youth development program implemented through before- and afterschool activities. BTF is a countywide partnership between United Way of Genesee County, the Flint Community Schools, the Genesee Intermediate School District and Genesee County's additional twenty school districts. BTF's before- and afterschool programs reinforce fundamentals learned during the school day and provide fun and creative learning experiences to kindergarten through ninth graders after school. The goal of the program is to meet the developmental needs of youths, building core assets and competencies that will ensure successful participation in adolescent and adult life.

The NCCE's most successful program currently is instituted at school districts throughout the country and is called the Afterschool Alliance. The following are three of many examples of the program's success noted in 2006:

In Modesto, California, more than three hundred children participated in Afterschool Alliance programs at Hanshaw Middle School and Mark Twain Junior High School each day, and for many of them, the opportunities the program provided were ones they could find nowhere else. John Ervin directs the afterschool program there.

Modesto's afterschool program, like so many others around the country, spared hundreds of working parents the burden of finding and paying for their children's supervision in the afterschool hours before parents get home from work. Nearly three-fourths of the schools' students were eligible for reduced-price lunches, and crime rates and gang participation was high. By providing safe, reliable and affordable supervision for children in the afterschool hours, Modesto's program served parents and children alike. "We've had students find their way because of this program," Ervin says. "They've changed their attitudes, pulled up their GPAs, abandoned the gangs and the streets and fixed their eyes on doing well in school."

Morgantown, West Virginia's Kaleidoscope afterschool and summer programs served approximately 10 percent of Morgantown's school-age population and received two grants from the 21st Century Community Learning Centers program. Project director Lynn Sobolov learned about collaboration at one of the National Center for Community Education's task force training sessions early in the grant cycle:

> *I came home and invited all the nonprofits in the area that have anything to do with afterschool to join a collaborative. Building sustainability and community support into a program from the beginning are keys to success. It is more than asking for money, it is making connections, building strong programs, generating trust, becoming visible. It's important to start that from the very beginning.*

After School for All members meet regularly to develop joint training projects, plan joint programming, arrange for visibility at community events and figure out how to find the resources to keep going. One of their plans included a community survey, upon which much of Kaleidoscope's programming is now based. Such community involvement is important to keep both parents and potential funding sources aware of the benefits of the program. "Don't rely on one pot of money," Sobolov said. "If you can become part of the landscape (a line item in someone's annual budget), you are well on your way to sustainability."

In St. Petersburg, Florida, students at John Hopkins Middle School, are learning about life under the sea, thanks to Project Tampa Bay, an initiative to introduce minority children to marine biology and its careers. The project is a community partner with Hopkins's 21st Century Community Learning Center afterschool program. "I have seen many kids turn around in this program," said Bruce Green, a program staff member. "We have one boy who was in trouble at school, his grades were down, his parents were worried about him…Now he's involved in the program, snorkeling and studying, and his grades and behavior have improved." The 21st CCLC afterschool program started when Hopkins Middle School first opened as a magnet school in 1999. "The school (and the afterschool program) have grown together, and it has proved to be an excellent partnership," said Irene Seybold, the 21st CCLC program manager. The 21st CCLC offers homework help and tutoring, as well as enrichment activities. "We make every effort to stay in constant contact with teachers and parents so that our afterschool homework help is connected directly to the curriculum programming," Seybold said. "We have found that about 45 percent of the kids in the program have improved their grades. Attendance and behavior has improved, too."

Back in Flint, the success of the programs caused the NCCE to outgrow the Crawford House location it had occupied since 1967, so it bought another historic mansion next door, the Burroughs House at 925 Avon, in 2002 to accommodate the growth. Budget issues forced NCCE to close in 2006. The Crawford and Burroughs Houses are now private residences.

In my own neighborhood, in 2006 I inquired with Coolidge Community School about its summer activities. Coolidge principal James Bracy informed me that Coolidge was hosting two summer programs, Summer Day Camp for children in the first through sixth grades and Tot Lot for children from ages four to six. I have fond memories of the Tot Lot program from my childhood, and Bracy was proud to say that Tot Lot was back that summer after a five-year absence. Some Flint schools offer summer basketball leagues. There are fees to register in these programs. The best-known local summer activity is the Flint Olympian Games, which Manley spearheaded when he complained to community school directors that there weren't enough summer programs for Flint youngsters in 1956. The Flint Olympian Games began at the old Northern High School with a modest series of athletic events. The games went international in 1957, when the CANUSA Games were added in partnership with Hamilton, Ontario. Flint hosts the CANUSA Games in even-numbered years and Hamilton in odd-numbered years.

Moving ahead to the summer of 2010, the Flint Community Schools continued to provide summertime activities, including Title I Pre-K and Tot Lot for young children; ACE (Academics, Citizenship and Effort) and Super Summer Success Reading for elementary school students; Shape Up, Go to Grade 7, Summer School and Enrichment and Go to Grade 9 for middle school students; and High School Summer School, High School 21st Century Programs and Driver's Education for high school students. The Flint Olympian and CANUSA Games continue. Child-care services are also offered during the summer, with the Rainbow Learning Program for children from two weeks to twelve years old. Additional programs are offered at other times of the year to both adults and youths to enrich both the mind and body.

So, despite the problems elsewhere in Flint that include the challenges the Flint Community Schools continue to face, the Community School movement that began in Flint is one success story that continues to bear fruit around the world.

Thanks to Dr. Gail Ganakas and Raven Lindsey of the Flint Community Schools and Coolidge School principal James Bracy.

The History of Flint's Alternative Newspapers

Since December 30, 1911, when the *Wolverine Citizen* published its final issue, the main source for local news was the *Flint Journal*. Toward the end of the *Wolverine Citizen*'s history, it was published by the *Flint Journal*, which advertised in that paper. The *Citizen*'s pages in the last issues were composed on the same galleys as the *Journal*'s, right down to the use of the *Flint Journal*'s name on the top of each page. While most of the references to the *Journal* were scraped off the top of each page, some managed to slip through in the *Citizen*'s pages. The *Wolverine Citizen* predated the *Flint Journal*; the *Citizen* was founded in 1850 as the *Genesee Whig* and changed its name to the *Wolverine Citizen* in 1856. The *Journal* was founded in 1876. This article chronicles publications that were published as alternatives to the *Flint Journal* and served the entire Flint population.

In 1910, a Socialist Labor publication called *Flint Flashes* was launched. George W. Starkweather, a machinist for the Weston-Mott Company, was encouraged by fellow members of organized labor to take over that paper, which was renamed the *Flint Weekly Review* in 1913. It proudly proclaimed on its masthead in 1923 that it was the "official newspaper of the City of Flint." The official newspaper status was voted by the Flint City Council, allowing the *Review* to publish exclusively all of the proceedings of the city council and all city notices. Nonreaders who were city taxpayers were able to get free copies of the *Review* containing official information from the city clerk's

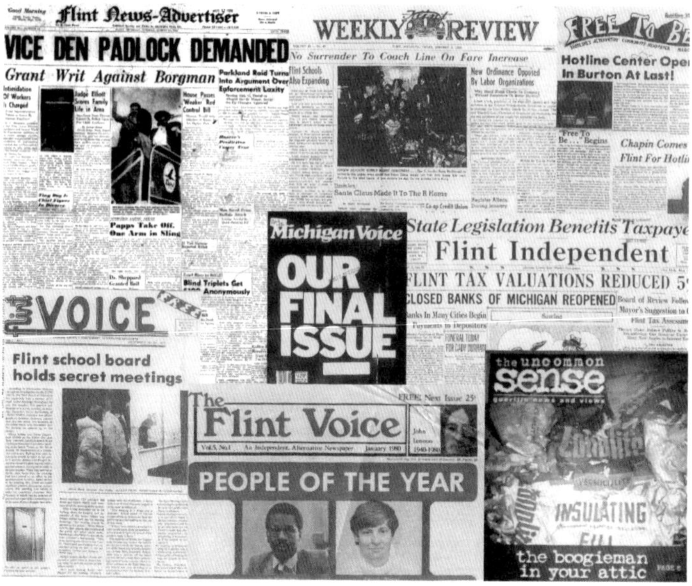

Alternative newspapers from Flint over the years.

office. The paper lost its official status with the city when Starkweather challenged incumbent mayor William McKeighan and ran for mayor in the Republican primary in 1929. Both he and McKeighan lost the primary to eventual winner Roy Brownell. Starkweather also published papers serving Swartz Creek, Lansing and Saginaw.

The *Flint Weekly Review* was also the official paper of the Flint Federation of Labor. Even though the *Review* was a labor publication, publisher Starkweather was a close friend of automotive leaders, including J.D. Dort, W.C. Durant, Walter Chrysler and his old employer, C.S. Mott. Starkweather promoted the interests of other groups in Flint, including the chamber of commerce and various civic organizations. As the local labor organizations evolved, the *Review* became the official publication of the Greater Flint Industrial Union Council CIO, which was later called the Greater Flint AFL-CIO Council. George Starkweather died on March 12, 1942, at age sixty-nine of a heart ailment. His widow, Bessie, took over as publisher. She sold the newspaper in 1951. It ceased publication with the June 27, 1963 issue, which was just four pages and was mostly ads. The end was abrupt, as there was no mention that this was the final issue. The Flint Weekly Review, Inc., was declared bankrupt on December 18, 1963.

A short-lived weekly was the *Flint Independent*, which began publication with the May 10, 1932 issue, became the *Flint Independent-Advertiser* with the

March 31, 1933 issue and ceased publication with the April 28, 1933 issue. It was formed by the merger of the *East Flint Beacon* and the *West Flint Telegram*. As the name implied, it was an independent newspaper that pledged to print the news impartially, supporting what it believed to be right and opposing what it believed to be wrong without regard to party politics. It was published by Independent Publishing Company. The printing office at 209 West First Avenue was taken over by another company, Advertisers Press, Inc.

Advertisers Press would launch the most ambitious early alternative paper, which lasted nearly twenty-five years. It was the *Flint News-Advertiser*, and it began publication with the December 22, 1933 issue and ended publication with the March 8, 1957 issue. It was published twice a week. The *News-Advertiser*, in its first issue, stated that it realized that a prevailing demand existed throughout the city for a news medium that would completely disseminate the important news of the community. It declared itself "a Flint newspaper for all Flint people." It declared itself to be an independent paper without affiliation with any political party, financial group, utility, manufacturing circle or any thing or person whatsoever. The sensationalist style of the news stories showed that this paper catered to the blue-collar readers of Flint. It ceased publication in 1957, citing rising costs. Advertisers Press is still in operation as a job printer, now located at 718 Harrison Street downtown.

The underground newspaper era was represented in Flint by the *Freedom Reader*, which was published from April 1971 to January 1973 and was funded by Mark Farner of Grand Funk Railroad fame. The editor of the *Freedom Reader* was Steve Lisuk.

The most famous local alternative newspaper publisher was Michael Moore, whose activism began as a student at Davison High School. He was elected to the Davison School Board in 1972, to the chagrin of the other board members. He survived a recall election but was defeated in seeking a second term. He founded the Davison Hotline, a crisis intervention center, and started his first newspaper, *Free To Be...* in 1977 as an extension of the hotline, which moved to Burton that same year. The name of the paper was changed to the *Flint Voice* in December 1977. The hotline's office was originally a former school leased by the Davison Schools to the Davison Hotline until the hotline was evicted. It moved into a house in Burton at 5005 Lapeer Road that doubled as the office for the newspaper. *Free To Be...* and the *Flint Voice* were published monthly and were free. The final free issue of the *Flint Voice* was the January 1981 issue. It became a twenty-five-cent biweekly with the February 6–19,

1981 issue. The *Flint Voice* expanded into the *Michigan Voice* later in 1981. While Moore was publishing the *Voice*, he also hosted a weekly radio show called *Radio Free Flint*. The *Michigan Voice* ceased publication with the April 1986 issue, when Michael Moore moved to San Francisco to become the editor of *Mother Jones* magazine. He was fired from *Mother Jones* after less than a year and returned to the Flint area about the time of massive General Motors layoffs. That inspired him to form Dog Eat Dog Films to make the documentary film *Roger & Me*. The film's unexpected success led to Moore's successful career producing feature films and TV shows, as well as writing bestselling books.

The next significant attempt at an alternative paper was the monthly *Uncommon Sense*, run by Matt Zacks. It was launched in January 2003. Beginning with the December 2005 issue, I contributed the local history pieces that have been compiled and updated for this book. Declining advertising revenue for the free publication led to it folding after the July 2007 issue was published.

Currently, the monthly free independent newspaper *Broadside*, founded in 2009 by Jon McCarron and a few friends, carries on the spirit of alternative newspapers.

I will conclude this chapter with a twist of irony. The Genesee District Library (GDL) received the *Flint Voice*, as proven by the mailing label on the February 6–19, 1981 issue (see page 182). But it did not allow the *Uncommon Sense* in its GDL locations. When the Linden Historical Society invited me to lecture at its meeting at the GDL branch at historic Linden Mills in July 2007, I brought over some back issues of the *Uncommon Sense*, which may have been the only time the publication was welcomed inside a GDL branch. Upstairs, some pieces I wrote for the Internet about Fenton- and Linden-area theaters were quoted in historical displays.

Update: The alternative publication *Broadside* invited this writer to contribute local history articles that would eventually be included in this book. After twenty-four issues were published, *Broadside* suspended publication in 2014. The reason cited was that the people involved had become too busy with other activities and projects.

Before Don, Before Woody, There Was Bill

In recent years, Flint has had two mayors who aspired to be boss mayors. They were Woodrow Stanley and Don Williamson. But neither of them could hold a candle to the most powerful mayor in the 150-year history of Flint. William McKeighan served as mayor on and off from 1915 to 1933. How powerful was he? So powerful that the city charter was revised in 1929 to try and take away his power.

William H. McKeighan was born in Cleveland, Ohio, on July 1, 1886. His family moved to Michigan when he was sixteen, living first in Saginaw and then in St. Charles, where he graduated from high school in 1906. During summer vacation and after school, the young McKeighan worked as a clerk in drugstores. After graduation, he studied to be a pharmacist and became registered as a certified pharmacist under Michigan law in 1907.

After traveling around the western states, in 1908 he settled permanently in Flint, where he was employed as a drug clerk for F.D. Baker & Son. Soon afterward, he partnered with two of his brothers, John and George, to establish their own drug business. The McKeighans would operate four drugstores throughout the city.

William McKeighan's political ambitions began early. In 1913, he was elected as alderman from the First Ward. On April 5, 1915, at the age of twenty-eight, he was elected to his first term as mayor of Flint. He did have bigger political ambitions. In 1914, he became the Republican nominee for

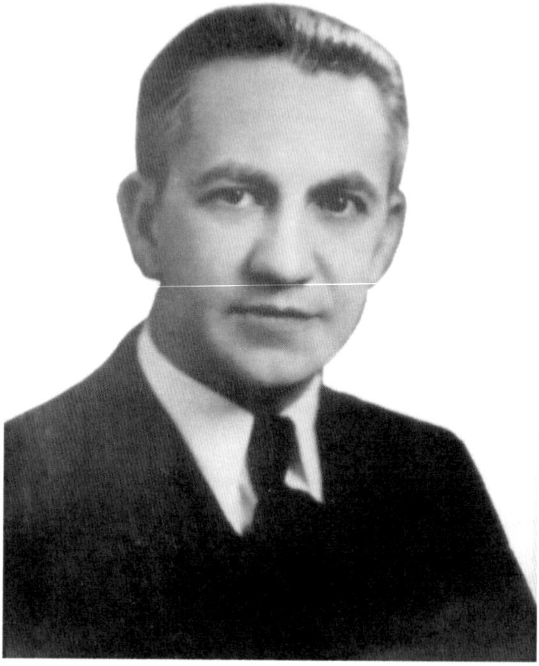

William McKeighan.

state senator but lost in the general election by a small majority. He was also an unsuccessful candidate for Genesee County sheriff in 1916 and 1927.

Through his pharmacies, McKeighan developed neighborhood contacts that would develop into a political machine that dominated Flint politics for several years. The machine either acted like a velvet glove or a mailed fist. McKeighan sought the support of newer Flint residents, who arrived to work at the expanding factories, including African Americans and recent immigrants. Arthur Hurand recalled that his father voted for McKeighan three times before he became an American citizen. He even sought the "kiddie vote" by passing out dimes to children at Lakeside Amusement Park along Thread Lake and Flint Park in northwest Flint. McKeighan also dominated Republican Party politics. Until 1940, McKeighan was one of three Republican politicians who together controlled the Michigan Republican Party. The other two were Edward Bernard of Detroit and Frank McKay of Grand Rapids. No GOP candidate for state office could be nominated without their consent.

Just like Don Williamson when he was much younger, William McKeighan had his run-ins with the law. His first arrest was in July 1914,

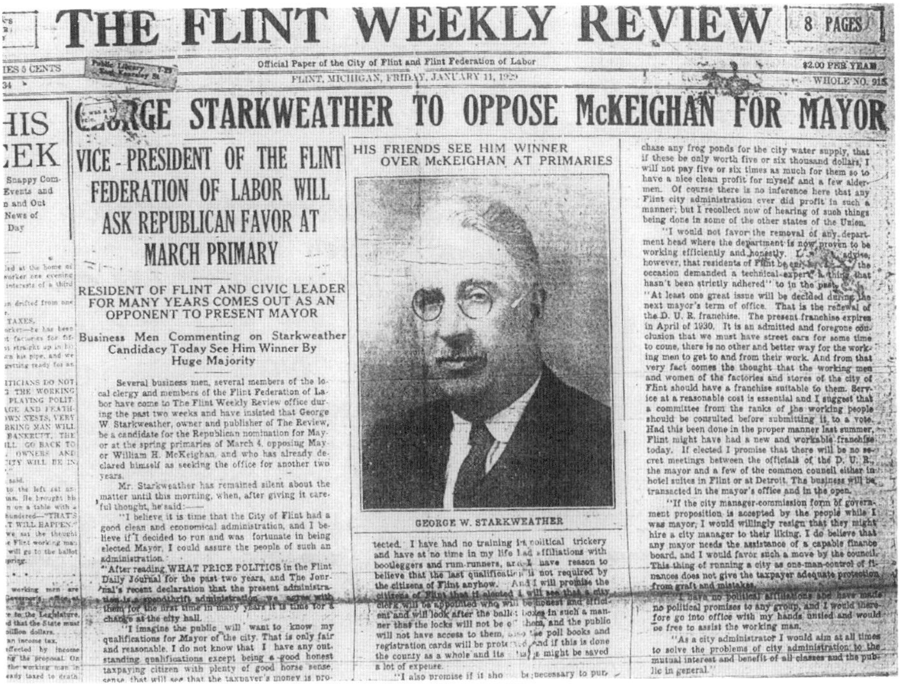

THE FLINT WEEKLY REVIEW

8 PAGES

Official Paper of the City of Flint and Flint Federation of Labor

FLINT, MICHIGAN, FRIDAY, JANUARY 11, 1929

$2.00 PER YEAR

WHOLE NO. 915

GEORGE STARKWEATHER TO OPPOSE McKEIGHAN FOR MAYOR

VICE-PRESIDENT OF THE FLINT FEDERATION OF LABOR WILL ASK REPUBLICAN FAVOR AT MARCH PRIMARY

RESIDENT OF FLINT AND CIVIC LEADER FOR MANY YEARS COMES OUT AS AN OPPONENT TO PRESENT MAYOR

Business Men Commenting on Starkweather Candidacy Today See Him Winner By Huge Majority

HIS FRIENDS SEE HIM WINNER OVER McKEIGHAN AT PRIMARIES

Several business men, several members of the local clergy and members of the Flint Federation of Labor have come to The Flint Weekly Review office during the past two weeks and have insisted that George W. Starkweather, owner and publisher of The Review, be a candidate for the Republican nomination for Mayor at the spring primaries of March 4, opposing Mayor William H. McKeighan, and who has already declared himself as seeking the office for another two years.

Mr. Starkweather has remained silent about the matter until this morning, when, after giving it careful thought, he said:—

"I believe it is time that the City of Flint had a good clean and economical administration, and I believe if I decided to run and was fortunate in being elected Mayor, I could assure the people of such an administration.

"After reading WHAT PRICE POLITICS in the Flint Daily Journal for the past two years, and The Journal's recent declaration that the present administration is a spendthrift administration, we agree with them for the first time in many years it is time for a change at the city hall.

"I imagine the public will want to know my qualifications for Mayor of the city. That is only fair and reasonable. I do not know that I have any outstanding qualifications except being a good honest taxpaying citizen with plenty of good horse sense, sense that will see that the taxpayer's money is protected. I have had no training in political trickery and have at no time in my life had affiliations with bootleggers and rum-runners, and I have reason to believe that the last qualification is not required by the citizens of Flint anyhow. And I will promise the citizens of Flint that if elected I will see that a city clerk will be appointed who will be honest and efficient and will look after the ballot boxes in such a manner that the locks will not be off them, and the public will not have access to them, also the poll books and registration cards will be protected and if this is done the county as a whole and its [illegible] might be saved a lot of expense.

"I also promise if it should be necessary to purchase any frog ponds for the city water supply, that if these be only worth five or six thousand dollars, I will not pay five or six times as much for them so to have a nice clean profit for myself and a few aldermen. Of course there is no inference here that any Flint city administration ever did profit in such a manner; but I recollect now of hearing of such things being done in some of the other states of the Union.

"I would not favor the removal of any department head where the department is now proven to be working efficiently and honestly. I [illegible] advise, however, that residents of Flint be [illegible] the occasion demanded a technical expert, a thing that hasn't been strictly adhered" to in the past.

"At least one great issue will be decided during the next mayor's term of office. That is the renewal of the D. U. R. franchise. The present franchise expires in April of 1930. It is an admitted and foregone conclusion that we must have street cars for some time to come, there is no other and better way for the working men to get to and from their work. And from that very fact comes the thought that the working men and women of the factories and stores of the city of Flint should have a franchise suitable to them. Service at a reasonable cost is essential and I suggest that a committee from the ranks of the working people should be consulted before submitting it to a vote. Had this been done in the proper manner last summer, Flint might have had a new and workable franchise today. If elected I promise that there will be no secret meetings between the officials of the D. U. R., the mayor and a few of the common council either in hotel suites in Flint or at Detroit. The business will be transacted in the mayor's office and in the open.

"If the city manager-commission form of government proposition is accepted by the people while I was mayor, I would willingly resign that they might hire a city manager to their liking. I do believe that any mayor needs the assistance of a capable finance board, and I would favor such a move by the council. This thing of running a city as one-man-control of finances does not give the taxpayer adequate protection from graft and mistakes.

"I have no political affiliations and have made no political promises to any group, and I would therefore go into office with my hands untied and would be free to assist the working man.

"As a city administrator I would aim at all times to solve the problems of city administration to the mutual interest and benefit of all classes and the public in general."

GEORGE W. STARKWEATHER

The *Flint Weekly Review* publisher unsuccessfully challenges McKeighan.

when he was accused of violating the local option law by selling a pint of brandy without a prescription. He was acquitted of that charge in 1915. It seemed he had help in his acquittal because the prosecutor in that case was a McKeighan man and didn't bother arguing the case. That was the first of several times McKeighan was charged with bootlegging, but he beat the rap each time.

There was just one time that McKeighan did time. In 1918, McKeighan was convicted of assault and armed robbery and sentenced to two to fourteen years in the Ionia Reformatory. The charge stemmed from a crap game in which friends of McKeighan claimed they were fleeced by crooked dice and McKeighan suggested that they strong-arm the suspected gambler. That gambler pressed charges against McKeighan as a result. McKeighan stayed in the Ionia Reformatory for just a week, and the Michigan Supreme Court later reversed his conviction. That week in jail, he later said, he slept in the warden's bedroom and dined with him daily. In 1941, he and McKay were accused of a $500,000 fraud through the use of real or pretended influence with the State Liquor Control Commission, but that case ended in a hung jury. A 1946 retrial ended in acquittal.

An extraordinary politician, McKeighan was the subject of both undying devotion and fanatical hatred. His enemies nicknamed him "Bootlegger." He returned as Flint mayor in 1922 and then returned again, serving a nonconsecutive term in 1927. Each time McKeighan served as mayor, he also presided over the Flint Common Council. The return of McKeighan as mayor usually led to upheaval, leading to court actions and hectic city council sessions. Once in office, he fired city employees right and left, made drastic changes and stirred up old feuds. When he returned as mayor in 1927, vital administrative personnel resigned, including the entire finance board. Others were fired. During his first three terms, he held the power of patronage and controlled the future of all city employees. One of the ways McKeighan got his way was by packing meetings with his own supporters, who filled the seats by arriving early. McKeighan's opponents had no choice but to stand. When votes were counted by people standing up, opponents who couldn't sit down or had no room to squat wound up voting against their wishes, despite their loud protests.

One of McKeighan's more controversial projects was the construction of Kearsley Dam, which was built to create Kearsley Lake, originally an 800-million-gallon reserve water supply. He allowed recreation on the lake to the disdain of the state health department.

In 1928, a recall election was held to try and remove McKeighan as mayor. The reasons for the recall were corruption, misuse of city funds and exorbitant water rates. McKeighan survived the recall attempt by a vote of 10,459 to 6,959. McKeighan was accused of buying the votes of African Americans, who unanimously voted to keep him.

After the unsuccessful recall campaign, a new charter was adopted by voters in 1929, changing from a strong mayor to a commission-manager form of government. Under this form of city government, the mayor became a figurehead chosen by the city council or commission from among themselves. The real power was in the hands of the city manager, who was hired and fired by a vote of the city council. This city charter was in effect until 1975, when the city switched back to a strong mayor form of government.

The new 1929 charter at first had little effect on McKeighan's dominant role. When he and his "Green Slate" of candidates won control of the city commission in 1931, the recently hired city manager, John N. Edy, immediately resigned, assuming the new city commission would fire him. The commission elected McKeighan mayor in 1931 and 1932 under the new charter. Fulfilling a campaign promise, he raised property taxes at a higher rate for chain stores and many businesses based out of town, causing many to appeal their tax assessments. These appeals were partially successful.

In 1932, McKeighan was a GOP candidate for governor of Michigan. But he lost the Republican primary to the incumbent governor, Wilber Brucker. Brucker was defeated by his Democratic challenger, William Comstock, under the weight of the Democratic Party landslide, which swept the Republicans out of power and made Franklin D. Roosevelt the president of the United States. McKeighan ran on a platform to repeal Prohibition. He relished Brucker's defeat, saying, "I really won by losing" because Roosevelt was also in favor of repealing Prohibition. In 1934, both William McKeighan and his brother, John McKeighan, decided not to seek reelection to the Flint City Commission. The McKeighan political machine was broken.

William McKeighan entered politics a poor man. Years later, newspapers reported that he was going to build a $7 million hotel on a block-long oceanfront lot he owned in Florida. In 1946, he was indicted by a one-man grand jury on bribe conspiracy charges in Macomb County, accused of being the payoff man in a multimillion-dollar gambling conspiracy. He left Michigan and remained for about eight years in Florida, claiming that he was unable to return because of ill health. It was said that McKeighan was secretly in Flint on a number of occasions during those years. In 1954, he was cleared of charges stemming from the indictments.

William McKeighan died of a stroke on September 15, 1957, in Miami, Florida, at the age of seventy-one. He was buried at Miami Memorial Park. The last McKeighan drugstore, at 1801 North Saginaw Street, closed about 1983 and was replaced by Pete's Market with the same phone number. That location is now a vacant lot.

The political machine that William McKeighan, his brothers and their supporters built was never rivaled in power before or since. He mentioned to an audience of supporters at one time, "I may make mistakes, I know I will. But they will be mistakes of the head and not of the heart." To give a final example of McKeighan's grip on city politics, an immigrant at the time answered the following questions posed by a naturalization examiner while seeking citizenship:

Q: Who makes the laws of our country?
A: Bill McKeighan.
Q: Who is the president?
A: Bill McKeighan.

In the 1920s and early 1930s, those answers in Flint were not too far off the mark.

The Flint Public Library has an extensive scrapbook of articles about William McKeighan.

THE GREAT FLOOD OF 1947

A combination of a spring snowstorm followed by heavy rains led to the worst flood in Flint history in 1947. It began with an early spring snowstorm in late March that paralyzed the city and even caused two trains to derail. But then came heavy rain, which, combined with melting snow, caused the Flint River to flood and effectively divided the city in two.

The snowstorm on March 25, 1947, brought Flint eleven inches of snow with drifts up to six to eight feet deep. The train derailments were both on the Pere Marquette (now CSX) belt line. One was near the Richfield Road crossing, and the other was near the Flint River trestle. By March 28, activities were back to near normal, but the temperature had risen, bringing forecasts of flooding. On April 1, the high temperature in Flint was forty-eight degrees. By noon the following day, the city had received one hundred phone calls reporting storm waters backing up sanitary sewers. By 1:15 p.m. that day, Flint had received 1.27 inches of rain, and Gilkey Creek had risen four feet overnight. On April 3, hundreds reported flooded basements.

On April 4, Flint received even more rain, and the Flint River rose thirty-two inches in a twenty-four-hour period. It was still raining the following day, and weather forecasters predicted record flooding as the Flint River rose an inch an hour but experienced a five-inch rise in one hour, overflowing Thread Lake.

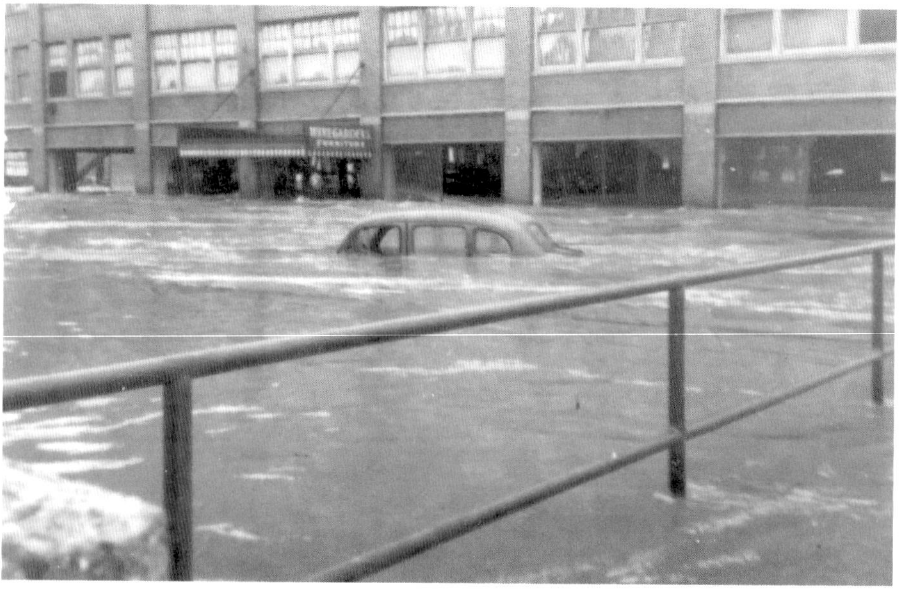

Winegarden's Furniture was hard hit by the flood. *Courtesy of Michael Madden of the Flint Public Library.*

On April 6, the flooding closed Saginaw Street downtown, and the following day, five blocks were flooded. The Flint River crested that day at 101½ inches above flood stage before gradually receding. The only bridges in the city that were still open at the peak of flooding were on Ballenger Highway on the west side and on Leith Street on the east side. On April 9, flood damage was estimated at $10,000,000 in 1947 dollars.

One of the hardest-hit businesses was Winegarden Furniture, whose plate glass windows were blown in by the floodwaters, causing furniture and appliances, including refrigerators, to float away and attracting looters, who were dealt with severely if they were caught. The National Guard assisted overworked police in guarding the flooded areas. When the floodwaters receded by April 10, the ground floor of the Winegarden Furniture store had completely buckled. The IMA Auditorium became an island. It was not flooded because workers had caulked all the doors, windows and other openings and mopped any floodwater that seeped in.

As insurance policies do not normally cover flooding, those affected had to rely on Red Cross aid and low-cost loans to recover from their losses. Flint was not alone with extensive flooding. Other parts of Michigan were

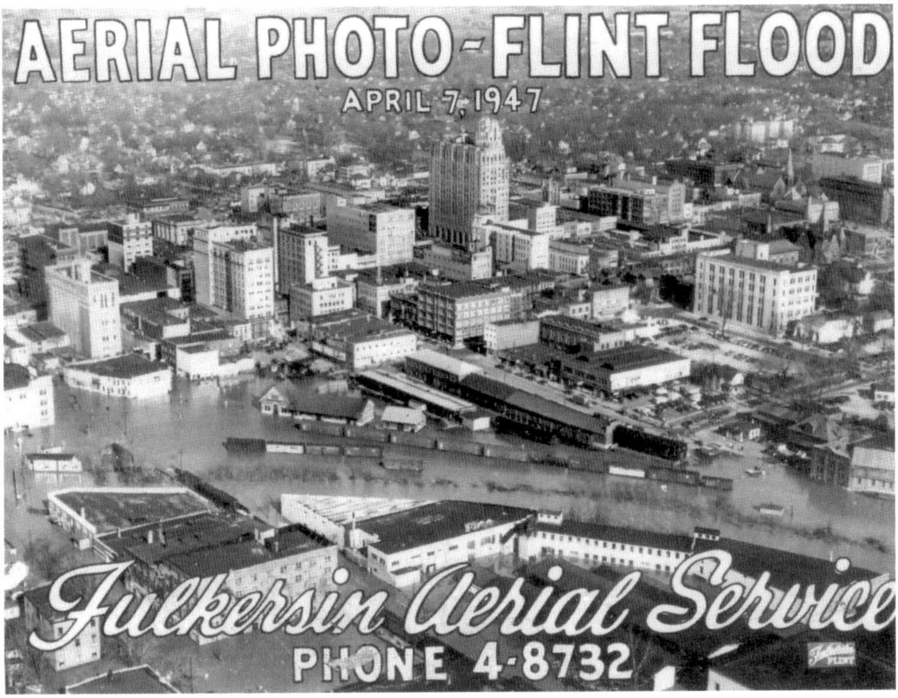

An aerial photo of the flood taken on April 7, 1947. *Courtesy of Michael Madden of the Flint Public Library.*

affected as well. When Henry Ford died on April 7, 1947, flooding along the River Rouge knocked out the powerhouse serving Ford's Fair Lane mansion in Dearborn, so it was lit by candlelight and oil lamps when Ford died.

The flood's effects were lasting, leading to flood control projects that became reality decades later. First was the purchase of land in 1950 along the Genesee and Lapeer county line near Columbiaville for construction of the Holloway Dam, which was completed in 1955 at a cost of $2,500,000. Holloway Reservoir flooded twenty-three hundred acres and backed up Flint River water for eight miles to create the largest body of water in the immediate area and the anchor for Holloway Reservoir Regional Park.

In 1966, a section of the Flint River bed from the Third Avenue/Sunset Drive Bridge to east of where Swartz Creek branches off near Atwood Stadium was completely paved by the Army Corps of Engineers, passing through the old "Chevy in the hole" manufacturing complex. City officials held out for something more attractive in the downtown area rather than the stark concrete bed.

In the early 1970s, the city began condemnation proceedings on land along the Flint River downtown to make way for the rest of the Army Corps of Engineers' flood control project. Along Saginaw Street, buildings on both sides of the Flint River between Water Street and First Avenue were purchased for demolition. They included the most unusual building constructed in Flint, the Center Building, which was built *over* the Flint River on the west side of the Saginaw Street Bridge. A snag involving a long-term lease on two billboards on the Center Building's roof delayed demolition of that building until the city settled with the billboard company. A new, higher Saginaw Street Bridge would also be built.

Riverbank Park was completed in 1979 and was a source of pride for the city with several water features, including an Archimedes' screw, which delivered water upward to feed the waterfalls. But nearly thirty years later, Riverbank Park is showing signs of wear and tear, as well as signs of neglect from budget cutbacks. The Archimedes' screw was dismantled, as it did not work and would be too expensive to repair; the Grand Fountain did not work either. It was suggested in a study that the lower sections of Riverbank Park be closed for safety and security reasons. The street level portions would remain open. Funds were found to restore Riverbank Park's water features in 2009.

But an even bigger concern is the Hamilton Dam, which was built in 1920 to raise the level of the Flint River to feed the Flint Water Plant three miles upstream. A recent inspection of the dam showed advanced deterioration. One of the floodgates was open, and the energy of the water flow was intense. Three of the six spillway gates do not work. If the dam were to fail, major downtown flooding would occur, endangering the public and leaching contaminants from adjacent brownfields into the river. The city is soliciting bids for either the refurbishing or replacement of Hamilton Dam. The extremely poor structural condition of the dam is such that, even though it provides direct access to University of Michigan–Flint buildings on both sides of the river, both sides are gated shut, closing the dam to pedestrian traffic. An estimate gave a replacement cost of $5.6 million for the dam in 2003. One idea proposed involves tearing down the dam and creating a whitewater rapids area.

Thanks to Michael Madden of the Flint Public Library for providing the flood photos.

Flint's Drive-In Theaters

On June 6, 1933, Richard Hollingshead opened the first drive-in movie theater in Camden, New Jersey. Thirteen years later, on August 29, 1946, Flint got its first taste of watching movies in the comfort of one's own car. Until the end of the 2008 season, the Flint area was totally unique in that it had two competing drive-in theaters in business. In many areas of the country, there are none left. It seems natural that in a city built on automobiles, we can still enjoy movies in our own private, comfortable seating areas. The difference now is that, instead of listening to the movie using the classic in-car speakers hanging from the speaker poles, you can now hear the movie in FM stereo on your car stereo system, as well as on a portable FM radio.

The last remaining drive-in theater still in operation is the U.S. 23 Drive-In Theatre with three screens at G-5200 Fenton Road in Mundy Township. The U.S. 23 opened in 1951 and was operated through 2008 by the Warrington family, who built the drive-in. It added a second screen in 1986. The original screen was destroyed in an arson fire in 1997 but was quickly replaced. The third screen was added in 2009.

There were once several drive-in theaters in operation in the Flint area. The first one was called the Drive-In Theatre and later dubbed the Dort Drive-In Theatre. It opened in 1946 at the corner of South Dort Highway and Atherton Road, where the Dort Mall now stands. It was co-founded

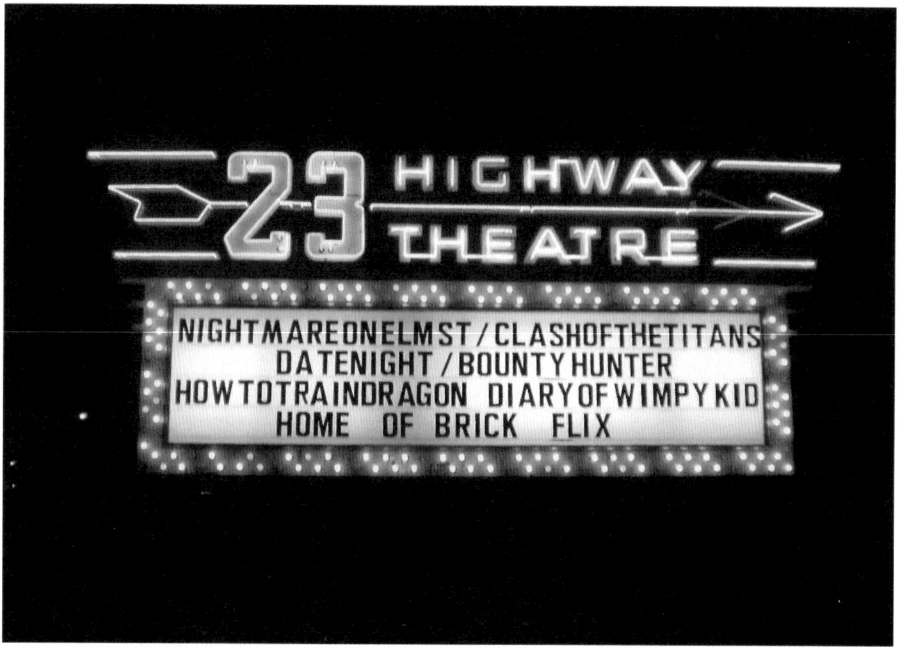

The U.S. 23 Drive-In marquee at night.

by William Oleksyn and William Rice. Oleksyn would later buy out Rice. In 1947, Oleksyn built a second drive-in located west of Flint on Corunna Road, appropriately called the West Side Drive-In Theatre. It was located where the HealthPlus office building now stands.

The success of Oleksyn's drive-ins inspired competition. Jerry Shinbach and Robert O. Fredley opened the Flint (later called North Flint) Drive-In Theatre at G-6101 North Saginaw Street north of Coldwater Road in 1948. Balancing out the location of drive-ins around town was Louis Warrington Sr. and Lee Stallard's aforementioned U.S. 23 Drive-In south of Flint in 1951. Warrington would later buy out Stallard's interest in that drive-in.

In 1955, all the drive-ins' huge screen towers had "wings" built to make the screens wider to accommodate wide-screen movies. Fenton got its own drive-in that same year when the Silver Drive-In was built at the corner of Silver Lake and Jennings Roads by Almond Sears. In 1956, Oleksyn built the Northland Drive-In at G-7192 North Dort Highway; it was the only drive-in built in the Flint area with a curved screen to better view wide-screen movies. Located where a now-closed wholesale auto auction facility is

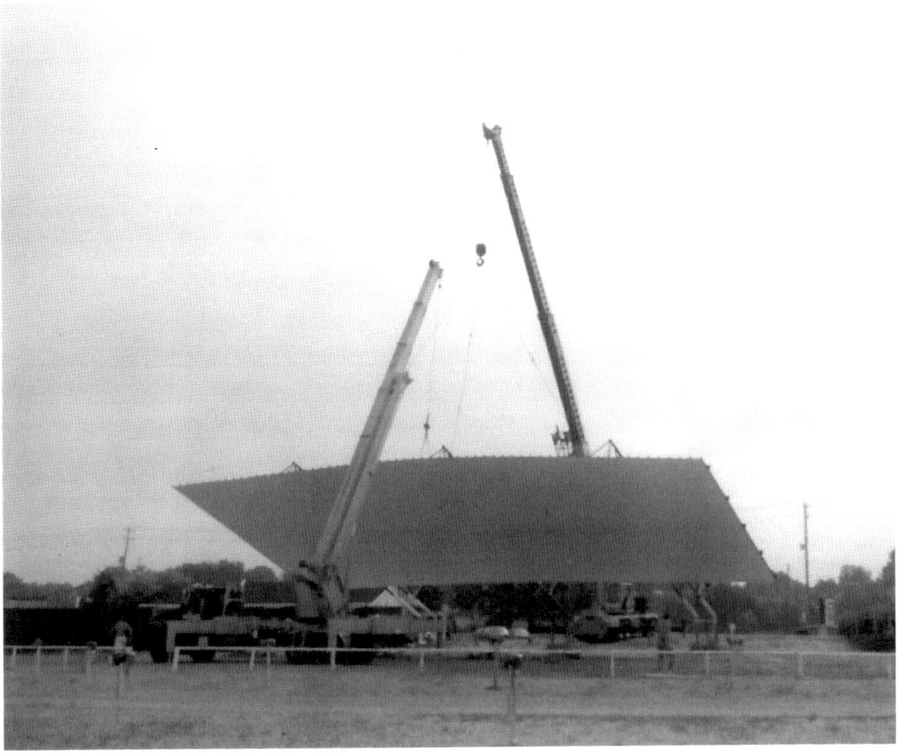

The 1997 U.S. 23 Drive-In replacement screen raising.

located, the Northland was also the first local drive-in equipped with in-car heaters, allowing the Northland to be open year round.

Because drive-in theaters require several acres of land, they were generally built outside of town where land was cheaper. So when the metropolitan areas grew, the land around the drive in theaters was developed, making the drive-in sites prime real estate. It soon reached a point where a drive-in's income was less than it would be if the land were put to other uses. That was the downfall of two of the drive-ins in the 1960s. The Dort was torn down in 1963 to make room for the first indoor shopping center, the Dort Mall, which Oleksyn developed. Oleksyn did build a replacement drive-in, the South Dort Drive-In, two miles south of the old location at the corner of South Dort Highway and Maple Avenue in Grand Blanc Township.

The other drive-in that was lost in the mid-1960s was the North Flint, which was replaced by a K-Mart store that has since closed. While the North

Flint Drive-In survived the 1953 Beecher tornado with only minor damage, it could not survive commercial encroachment.

In 1964, Oleksyn sold his drive-in theaters to the W.S. Butterfield Theatres chain, which was the dominant theater operator in Flint at that time. The theater chain that would eventually overtake Butterfield Theatres' dominance of the Flint area opened its first theater, a drive-in, in 1973. National Amusements, led by Sumner Redstone, built the Miracle Twin Drive-In near the M-21 (now I-69) Belsay Road exit. The Miracle Twin was a year-round drive-in, like the aforementioned Northland, South Dort and the retrofitted U.S. 23. But by the late 1970s, high energy prices and a decline in the youth population forced the year-round drive-ins to go seasonal one by one. The U.S. 23 was the first to go seasonal in 1972. The Northland was closed for the season during the winter of 1975–76. The co-owned South Dort closed the following year for the winter of 1976–77. The last holdout was the Miracle Twin, but it started closing for the season in the winter of 1979–80.

The 1980s was a bad decade for drive-ins in general, as many of them closed for redevelopment. Butterfield Theatres sold most of its theaters in 1985. Two of its drive-ins, the South Dort and West Side, were sold for redevelopment. The South Dort's prefabricated 60- by 120-foot screen tower was salvaged and sold to the U.S. 23 Drive-In, which built a 38- by 76-foot second screen using the tower parts. The U.S. 23 had planned to eventually build a third screen, but the 1997 fire that destroyed the U.S. 23's original screen tower led to the construction of the replacement screen using the remaining tower parts. The U.S. 23's twin screens 1 and 2 were both derived from the South Dort Drive-In's screen. The Mass Transportation Authority's Grand Blanc facility, Creative Foam Corporation and John Deere Landscapes, now occupies the former South Dort Drive-In site. The Northland stayed opened for two more seasons before a decline in business led to that drive-in's permanent closing in August 1986. In terms of booking movies, the single-screen Northland was at a competitive disadvantage compared to the Miracle Twin and U.S. 23 Drive-Ins, each with two screens. The Silver Drive-In in Fenton also closed permanently in 1986. It was torn down the following year to make way for the Silver Lake Village development.

In January 2008, second-generation U.S. 23 owner Louis Warrington Jr. suffered a heart attack that left him homebound. His wife, Diane, ran the drive-in that year, but there were concerns about its future. After Labor Day 2008, the Miracle Twin Drive-in closed permanently, as did National Amusements' other remaining drive-in in Louisville, Kentucky. Warrington died on February 18, 2009. There was talk of the family running the drive-in for one final year before selling it. But they decided not to sell. Lou Warrington III, who lives in Texas, signed a five-year lease with another operator, who began making improvements to the U.S. 23 Drive-In Theatre before it opened for the 2009 season. As you enter the drive-in to take in a movie, you will notice that the neon attraction board was fully restored, including the chaser lights and animated arrow, both of which had not worked for several years. The in-car speakers were removed; FM stereo radio sound is used for all movies. The screens were painted, new box offices were built, the projection equipment was fully automated, the restrooms were improved and the refreshment stand was renovated. The third screen was added in August 2009, built using used shipping containers.

The U.S. 23 Drive-In Theatre shows first-run double features on its three screens and is open on weekends from April to Memorial Day. It is open nightly through Labor Day and on weekends through October.

Update: The Flint area's last remaining drive-in theater, the US 23 Drive-in Theatre, was equipped with digital projectors in 2013 and continues to draw moviegoers each summer. The Back to the Bricks annual August series of events is kicked off each year by Bricks Flicks, which features classic cars—often overflowing the drive-in—a DJ and a free automotive-themed classic movie showing at dusk. Meanwhile, all structures except the two screen towers and attraction boards were torn down in 2012 at the vacant Miracle Twin Drive-in Theatre in Burton. Vegetation is growing in cracks in the asphalt field where the speaker poles still stand. The property at this writing is listed for sale at an asking price of $1.6 million.

The History of Flint's Rescue Missions

During the year-end holiday season, when we think about how fortunate we are, we should also think about those who are not so fortunate. One of the leading movements serving the down-and-out in communities are the rescue missions.

The rescue mission movement was founded by Jerry McAuley, an Irish immigrant who never knew his father and whose mother never took care of him. Growing up on the streets of New York City, living as a thief, he was sent to Sing Sing Prison in 1857 at age nineteen to serve a fifteen-year sentence for a crime he said he didn't commit. McAuley sought to straighten out his life and began to follow the rules given to him. He began to read the Bible in prison. He was paroled in 1864 at age twenty-six. He associated himself with avowed Christians, who would influence his direction in a positive manner. One of them was an ex-prostitute named Maria, whom he married. His benefactors and personal experience, as well as "a vision," allowed him and his wife to found the first rescue mission at 316 Water Street in New York City in 1872. McAuley died in 1884 of tuberculosis, which he contracted at Sing Sing.

Other rescue missions were founded in other large cities, and an association of rescue missions was founded in 1913; it is now called the Association of Gospel Rescue Missions.

Flint's boomtown origins meant that there were not that many have-nots until the Stock Market Crash of 1929 brought about the Great Depression

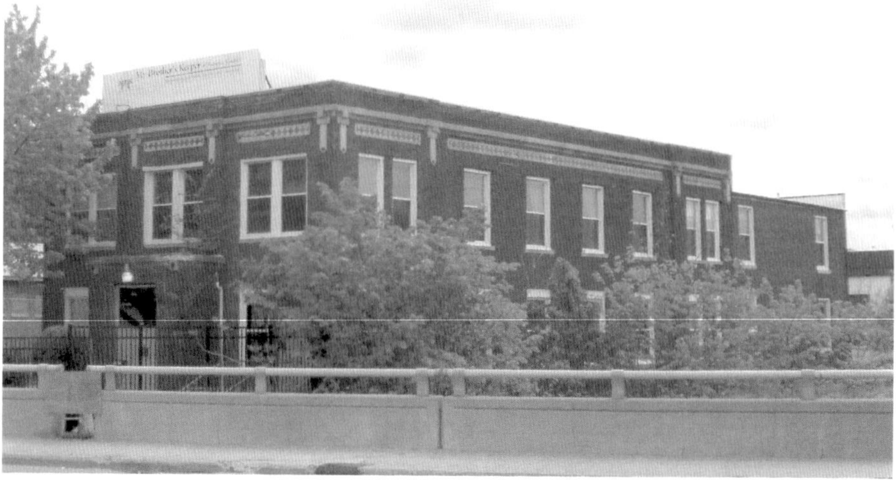

The former Rescue Mission of Flint, now My Brother's Keeper of Genesee County.

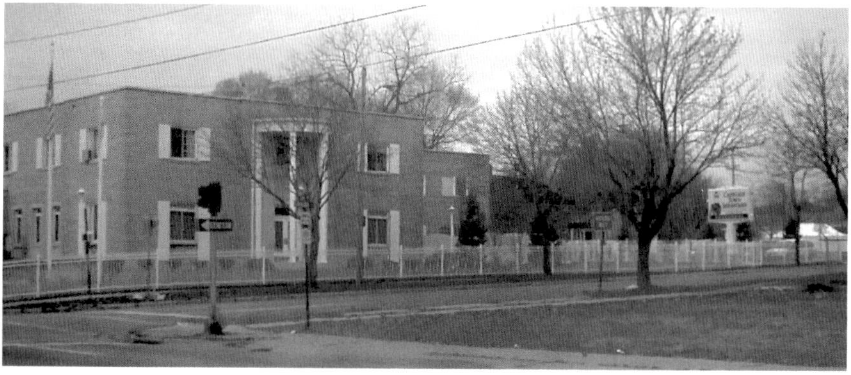

Carriage Town Ministries.

and hard times. This led to the formation of Union Rescue Mission, Inc., at the former St. Joseph Hospital location at the old Stockton House (now the Stockton Center at Spring Grove office building and museum), at 720 Ann Arbor Street, about 1938. The first superintendent was Carl H. Rhodes. In 1939, Mrs. Peggy Gearhart was the mission's matron. The Reverend L. Fred Peter took over by 1941. America's entry into World War II after the December 7, 1941 Pearl Harbor attack effectively ended the Great Depression and led to labor shortages as a result of the large number of able-bodied men called into military service. This also meant that even the lowliest of down-and-out people were able to find work and a place to live, negating the need for the Union Rescue Mission. The mission sold the Stockton House, which became a home for the aged.

The end of the war also ended the labor shortage as the troops arrived home, and the least qualified were once again on the streets. Local churches banded together in 1949 and made contact with other rescue missions around the state. An office building at 101 Smith Street (now 101 North Grand Traverse) was purchased for $17,500, with the $5,000 raised for the down payment.

The founding superintendent, Reverend John Schaich, was a "beloved brother in Christ" who loved souls and was not afraid of hard work. He was saved at the Rescue Mission in Grand Rapids and was recruited to start the Rescue Mission of Flint, which was dedicated on October 8, 1950, after the office building was renovated to develop dormitory rooms for the homeless, a kitchen to feed them and a chapel to hold services. Reverend Schaich served as superintendent for nearly thirty years. In the mid-1970s, he even hosted a radio show on Sunday mornings on WTRX. After Reverend Schaich's retirement, Reverend Jerry L. Peaster took over in 1979.

As the Mission's clientele grew larger, it found itself requiring more space. The Rescue Mission's Grand Traverse location became too small to serve the growing number of people in need of its services. So in 1986, despite opposition from residents concerned that it would attract more homeless people to the neighborhood, the mission purchased the former Groves Funeral Home at 605 Garland Street in the Carriage Town area. After the building was renovated, the renamed Carriage Town Mission was dedicated in November 1987. The new facility included a clothing distribution area twice as large as the old Grand Traverse location, a men's dormitory with sixty beds, more permanent housing for up to nine men for up to six months in the drug or alcohol abuse rehabilitation and job training programs, a dining room seating one hundred, a chapel seating more than one hundred, a day room for men to keep warm during cold weather and a garage for mission vehicles and plenty of parking for staff, volunteers and visitors. The former location on Grand Traverse became the Harvest House women's shelter, which closed in 2006 and is now a homeless shelter operated by My Brother's Keeper of Genesee County.

In 1991, the Carriage Town Mission purchased the Knights of Columbus building at 705 Garland Street, one block away, to provide a shelter for women and children. The renovated building, called the Family Center, features twelve separate bedrooms for women and children, a dormitory for two to six women with no children, a family apartment for an entire family, a living area with a kitchen, a playroom, a library, a clinic and a youth center, including a gym. Both the original Carriage Town Mission building and the Family Center are completely fenced in. As a result of the expanded services the mission offered to the homeless, Carriage Town Mission changed its name to Carriage Town Ministries in 1993. In 1994, Carriage Town Ministries added the Innovative Learning Center to provide enhanced teaching facilities to the ministries' clients, allowing them to develop marketable skills and gain employment.

In 2000, Reverend Robert Sweeney became executive director after Reverend Peaster's retirement. Mrs. Lois St. Clair took over in 2004. After she retired in 2009, Dallas Gatlin became executive director. Carriage Town Ministries is an official 501c3 nonprofit organization and a member of both the Association of Gospel Rescue Missions and the Evangelical Council for Financial Accountability. It offers its services to anyone in need with no barriers or restrictions. While Carriage Town Ministries is a faith-based organization, it does not force participation in religious activities, but clients are strongly encouraged to participate if they wish to be fed there. The ministries serve more than forty-three thousand meals each year, offered more than twenty-five thousand nights of safe lodging to clients in 2005 and give away, free of charge, an average of more than eleven thousand pieces of clothing each month.

Thanks to Carriage Town Ministries. Information about the earlier Union Rescue Mission was from Polk's Flint City Directories.

Flint's Cartoon Mascots

The trademarks and registered trademarks depicted in this article are the properties of their respective owners. Illustrations were rendered by Randy Zimmerman.

The Dawn Donuts Do-Boy

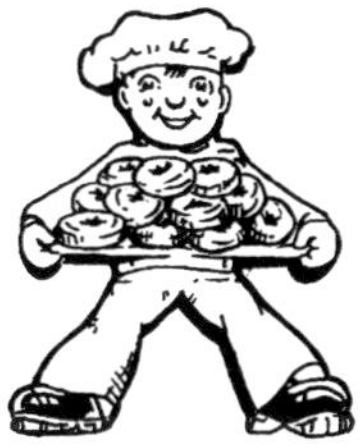

It started with a single bakery in Jackson, founded in 1920, which made donuts so good that competitors asked for its prepared mix. Dawn Donut Company closed the bakery and started America's first wholesale mix company, supplying batter mix to bakeries. One of its customers was the Flint Baking Company on Industrial Avenue, founded in 1928 by Julius Hurand. It would evolve into Buttercup Bakeries. Julius's son, Arthur, joined the business after World War II. Arthur started a side business called Do-Boy Donuts, borrowing the Dawn Donuts mascot, which was introduced in 1926. In 1955, Dawn Donut Company gave the Hurands retail and franchising rights to the Dawn Donuts name. That started the successful Dawn Donuts chain of donut shops, which, at its peak, had sixty stores in Michigan. Dawn Donut Systems, Inc., sold the donut shops to Dunkin' Donuts in 1991. What is now Dawn Food Products, Inc., a global bakery supply company still based in Jackson, was given back the retail and franchising rights to the Dawn Donuts name, as well as the do-boy mascot, for which it still owns the registered trademark. Dawn franchisees that refused to convert to Dunkin' Donuts were allowed to keep the Dawn Donuts name, but no new Dawn Donuts franchises will be granted. There are three Dawn Donut locations left in the area: at the corner of Clio and Pasadena in Flint, at the corner of Perry and Saginaw in Grand Blanc and at the corner of Hill and Fenton in Grand Blanc.

MR. C.B.

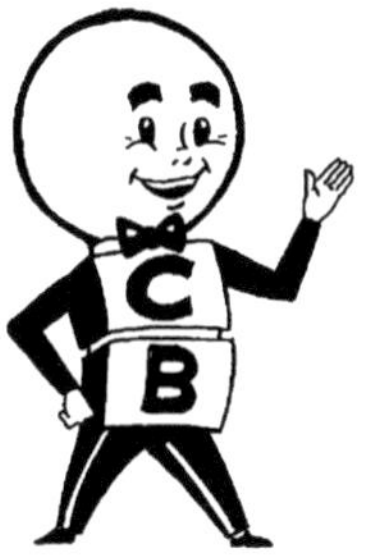

Ever since the Citizens Bank weather ball was built atop the Citizens Bank Building in 1956, it has served as the symbol of Citizens Bank. As a symbol, the weather ball went through several incarnations. My favorite was the 1960s stout looking Mr. C.B. which replaced the original skinny Mr. Weather Ball (see page 152) in which the weather ball sprouted arms, legs and a face. This smiling friendly symbol also adorned dime folders for children to collect three dollars worth of dimes.

GENNY THE AUTOMATIC TELLER

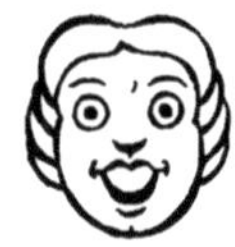

Four name changes ago, in 1977, Genesee Bank introduced ATMs. It wanted a human face to represent its ATMs, so it introduced Genny as the mascot to adorn the ATMs. NBD bought the bank in the mid-1980s, and Genny disappeared when Genesee Bank became NBD Genesee Bank. The loosening of Michigan banking laws later that decade caused the Genesee name to disappear all together. In 1998, NBD's parent company merged with Ohio-based Bank One and adopted the Bank One name. In 2004, J.P. Morgan Chase bought Bank One, and in 2006, the Bank One signs were replaced by Chase signs. We miss Genny.

The Kewpee Doll

Founded in 1923 by Sam "Old Man Kewpee" Blair, the Kewpee Hotel hamburger stand developed into a landmark restaurant with a Kewpee doll mascot. Its hamburger wrappers bore the slogan, "Hamburg, pickle on top! Makes your heart go flippity flop!" At its peak, before World War II, there were two hundred Kewpee restaurants around the country. A second Kewpee location opened in 1951 in downtown Flint at the former Vernor's outlet, which is now the flagship Halo Burger location.

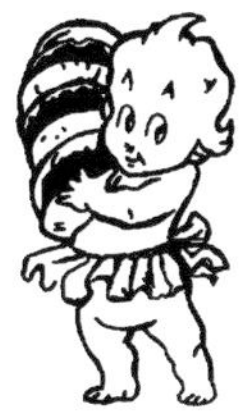

The Halo Burger Cow

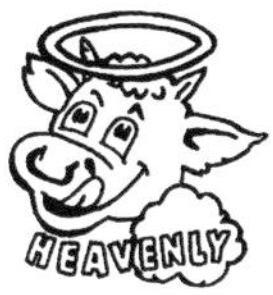

Bill Thomas began working at Kewpee in 1938. When Kewpee owner Sam Blair retired, Thomas took it over, leasing the restaurant from Blair. Thomas became full owner of the local Kewpee operations in 1958, but he couldn't afford the rights to the Kewpee name and logo. The rights were sold to a man in Ohio, where Kewpee is still operating in Lima. Kewpee, Inc., of Lima, Ohio, still owns the registered trademark. When the owner of the Kewpee name demanded full franchise fees and a percentage of the profits in 1967, Bill Thomas changed the name of his restaurants to Bill Thomas's Halo Burger. He also introduced his "heavenly" angelic cow mascot on the new signs, replacing the Kewpee signs. Halo Burger itself has become a destination for both locals and visitors seeking a great hamburger, with nine locations in the Flint area.

Woody the Vernor's Gnome

Downtown Flint is home to one of the last surviving advertising signs for Vernor's Ginger Ale. First painted in 1932, the three-story mural on the north wall of the Greater Flint Arts Council building next to Halo Burger (originally the Vernor's retail store and sandwich shop) depicts Vernor's mascot

gnomes working out of a castle and stacking oak barrels of gingery Vernor's syrup. The gnome, named Woody, was created in the early 1900s by James Vernor II and artist Nobel Fellows. He usually appeared along with an oak barrel, as if guarding a treasure. The mural has become a recognizable Flint landmark. It was restored twice in recent years, in 1979 and 2001.

SLIM CHIPLY

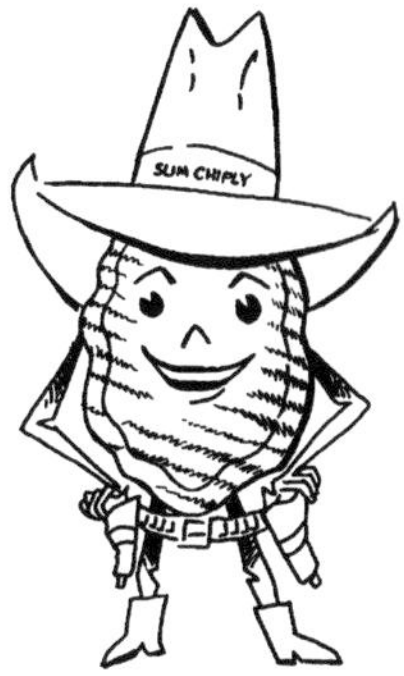

For thirty years from about 1962 to 1992, this pistol-packin' potato chip graced the bright red bags of Paramount Potato Chips. The company was headed by president Robert N. Johnson, and the story goes that the Slim Chiply mascot was inspired by his son, who was a fan of westerns. The plant was located at 2727 Lippincott Boulevard. Flintites with long memories can probably still sing the old Paramount Potato Chips jingle, which was sung by Slim Chiply himself. The mascot told everyone to reach for Paramount Potato Chips. When the company went bankrupt as a result of the Hamady supermarkets bankruptcy and closing, as well as an expensive sex discrimination legal settlement, Better Made Snack Foods of Detroit took over the assets. Both Better Made and Bay City–based Made Rite Potato Chips took over as much space as possible on the store shelves to gain better exposure. Made Rite was sold to Better Made in 1994, and the Made Rite name was eventually phased out. Better Made Potato Chips, which still owns the Paramount name and Slim Chiply even though they are now dormant, is on local snack food shelves.

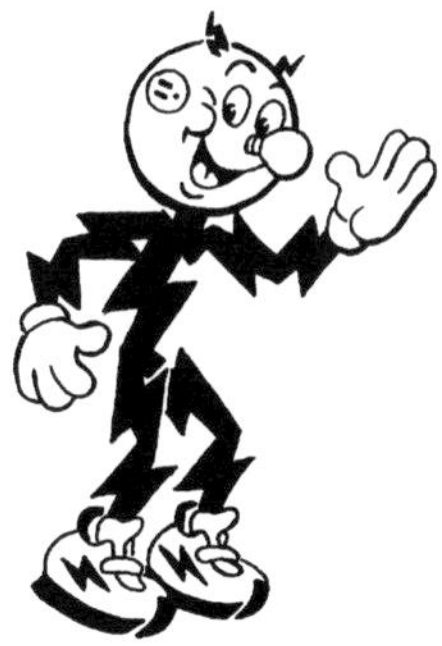

REDDY KILOWATT

In 1926, the Alabama Power Company introduced Reddy Kilowatt as a cartoon spokesman for electricity. About two hundred other electric utilities adopted him as their mascot, including Consumers Power Company, which used him through the 1960s.

Reddy Kilowatt appeared in comic books, in educational filmstrips and in an animated cartoon. He was even made into a doll. He fell out of favor in the 1970s, when energy conservation became the norm. Today, he is a registered trademark of Reddy Kilowatt Corporation, a unit of Xcel Energy, of Minneapolis, Minnesota.

JELL E. BEAN

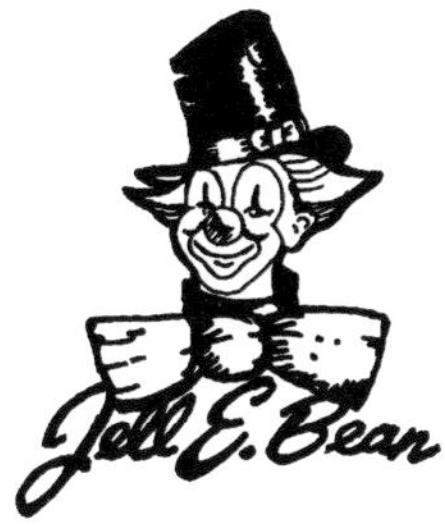

When pizza parlors developed into entertainment centers with arcade games and robotic entertainers such as Chuck E. Cheese, veteran hotel manager Cass Opyt (unable to obtain a local franchise for a national chain) decided to develop one of his own called Circus Time Pizza on South Dort Highway in the Dort Mall (called the Small Mall at the time). It opened in March 1983. Local radio station owner Neil J. Mason was Opyt's partner in the venture. The mascot was Jell E. Bean the clown, who appeared not only in Circus Time Pizza's logo but also as a huge sign, making him look as if he was holding on to the signpost. Opyt had plans to open additional locations and offer franchises. Unfortunately, Dort Highway was in decline at that time, and the mall had become a magnet for car cruisers that sometimes got rowdy. Opyt attempted to diversify the entertainment offerings by having Circus Time After Dark, featuring popular comedians. But after a year or so, he ran out of money, and Circus Time Pizza went bankrupt. The equipment and fixtures were auctioned off, and the Jell E. Bean clown sign was purchased by Skateland Arena on North Dort Highway in Mt. Morris, where the clown hung on to the side of the Skateland Arena sign for many years. That sign was sold to Dort Mall owner and noted collector Bob Perani, who had it restored at Signs by Crannie. The Jell E. Bean sign is now in the Dort Mall's parking lot. The Circus Time Pizza location is today Big Lots.

YANKEE STORES' UNCLE SAM

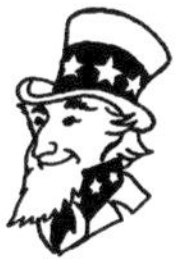

In the 1950s, Joseph Megdell and Wilbert Roberts were building a successful general merchandise store chain called Yankee Stores. Uncle Sam, with his famous red, white and blue patriotic hat, was their mascot. By the late 1950s, Uncle Sam was gone, but his hat remained as Yankee Stores' symbol. Megdell and Roberts sold the chain in 1965, and Megdell left in 1967. After Megdell left, the chain began a gradual decline, and the stores, later renamed Zodys, closed for good at the end of 1974.

THE MR. BREAD BUNS

The cartoon buns have graced the Mr. Bread delivery trucks since Mr. Bread was founded in 1977 by two veterans of the bakery business with one truck and a rented building in Flint. The business has grown and now has seven trucks and a sales territory stretching to eight counties. It serves three hundred regular customers. Mr. Bread's flagship product is the seven-inch Coney bun sold to restaurants. It's located on Davison Road near Dort Highway.

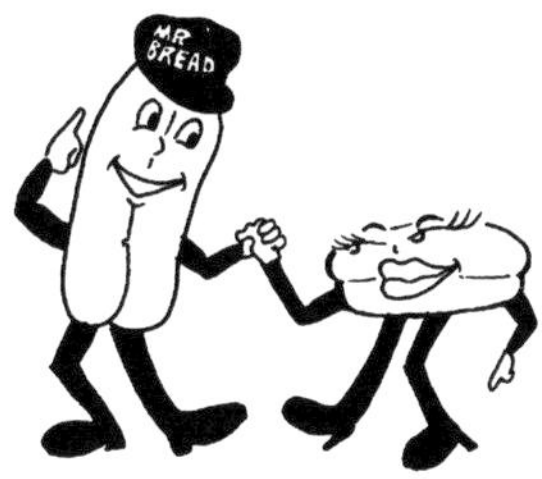

MUFFLER MAN

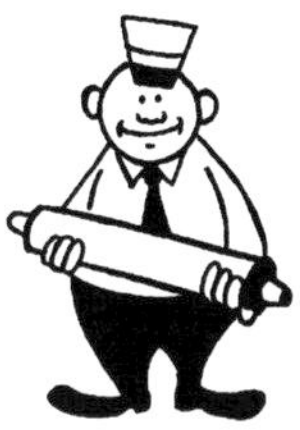

Muffler Man was founded in 1968 and developed into a large chain of auto repair shops, but not without problems. When Muffler Man decided to expand outside Michigan, it discovered other muffler shops using the Muffler Man name. To avoid expensive legal battles, it decided to call its locations outside Michigan Rainbow Muffler, using a rainbow tree design. The tree design accompanies the Muffler Man mascot at Muffler Man locations in Michigan. Muffler Man/Rainbow Muffler is still headquartered in the Flint area on Holiday Drive in Flint Township. The Muffler Man name, mascot and rainbow tree design are registered trademarks of Muffler Man, Inc.

Sparky the AC Spark Plug Horse

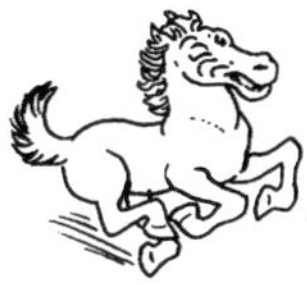

From the 1920s through the 1950s, AC Spark Plug had a winking horse mascot that was featured in advertisements of the era. In early ads, he was shown in a bathtub, and he was even made into a promotional statuette. A temporary exhibit at the Sloan Museum—which paid tribute to AC Spark Plug after spark plug production in Flint was ended by AC's successor company, Delphi—showed examples of Sparky the Horse. The old AC factory complex on Dort Highway is now gone.

Ron's Ice Cream Cone, "The King"

A longtime south side Flint landmark was opened at $3122\frac{1}{2}$ Fenton Road in 1982 by Don R. Schmidt. His "The King" ice cream cone mascot was painted on the walls of the stand. It has since expanded to occupy the whole building at 3122 Fenton Road, across from Cody School, and has added pizza to its menu. A more professionally designed mascot adorns the electric sign, which coexists with the charming, painted-on mascot at the restaurant.

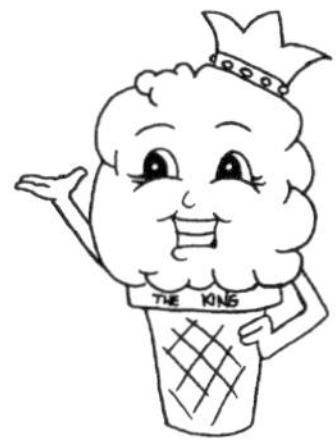

"Carl" of Carl's Best Beans & Greens Restaurant

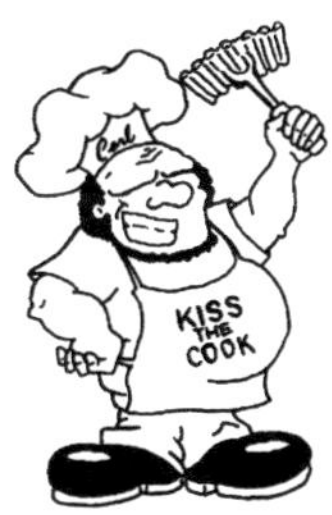

A locally owned restaurant at 1901 South Dort Highway south of I-69 opened in 2005 and had a mascot of Carl himself serving up some tasty ribs. The restaurant building went through several different owners over the years since it was built in the mid-1970s as Sambo's. When Sambo's folded, it was a Big Boy until that, too, closed. Carl's Best is now closed as well.

WFBE's Buzby the Bee

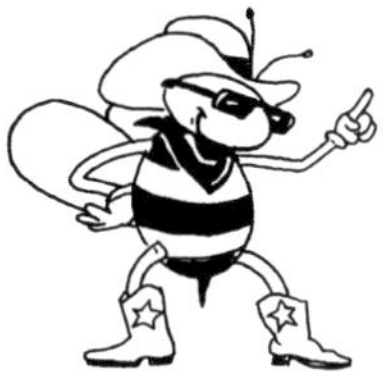

In 1997, the Flint Community Schools couldn't afford to operate public radio station WFBE 95.1 FM anymore, and it sold the station to a commercial operator, which retained the WFBE call letters. In October 1997, B95, with a country music format, was launched, with a cartoon bee wearing a cowboy hat and boots as its mascot. The mascot was clearly derived from the station's call letters. A listener contest gave the bee a name: Buzby.

WRSR's Fox

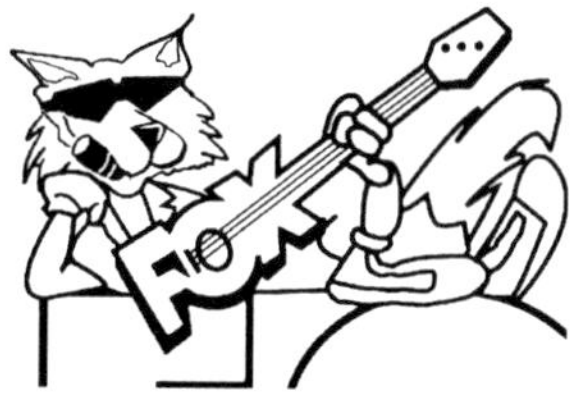

In 2000, radio station WRSR, licensed to Owosso, adopted a classic rock format using as its identifier "The Fox," with a cartoon fox holding a guitar shaped like the word "fox" as its mascot. The station itself was originally WOAP-FM in 1965. It was changed to WMZX in 1989, then WAHV in 1996 and finally WRSR in 1998.

Honorable Mentions Go to Two Mascots that Could Not Be Located

Merlin's Retreat was a vegetarian restaurant located at the corner of Detroit (now MLK) and Fifth Avenues. It was in operation in the 1980s. It had a mascot of Merlin the wizard for several years after it closed.

Quality Cat from the GM Truck & Bus Assembly Plant was made famous by Ben Hamper in his 1991 book, *Rivethead.*

Mascots were nominated by the Uncommon Sense *staff and rendered by Randy Zimmerman.*

Update: The WFBE bee mascot was retired in 2014 when the station changed its branding from B95 to Nash FM. The Halo Burger cow, which was retired after Dortch Enterprises took over, was brought back in 2016 by new owner Halo Country after it was given a makeover.

Early TV in Flint, Or the Lack of It

Television was slow to arrive in Flint. Detroit had three TV stations in the late 1940s, but none had strong signals at that time. The first good TV signal Flint received was from Lansing when WJIM-TV (now WLNS) channel 6 first signed on in 1950 with programming from all the major TV networks but primarily affiliated with CBS.

In 1952, the Federal Communications Commission created a TV allocation table that assigned three TV channels to Flint: VHF channel 12 and two UHF channels, channel 16 and noncommercial channel 28. There were three competing applicants for channel 12: WFDF radio owner Trebit Corp., W.S. Butterfield Theatres and WJR radio owner Goodwill Stations, Inc. Channel 28 was awarded to Trans-American Television Corp. of Philadelphia, with the call letters WCTV, but it never got the station on the air. Channel 28 would not get on the air until the University of Michigan–Flint's WFUM first signed on in 1980.

As for channel 16, the Trendle-Campbell Broadcasting Corporation, owner of WTAC radio (now WSNL), was the only applicant, so it built WTAC-TV, an ABC affiliate. The owners were George W. Trendle (creator of *The Lone Ranger*) and H. Allen Campbell. The station signed on for the first time on Thanksgiving Day, November 26, 1953, from studios and offices at 2302 Lapeer Road, with a 467-foot broadcast tower behind the studios.

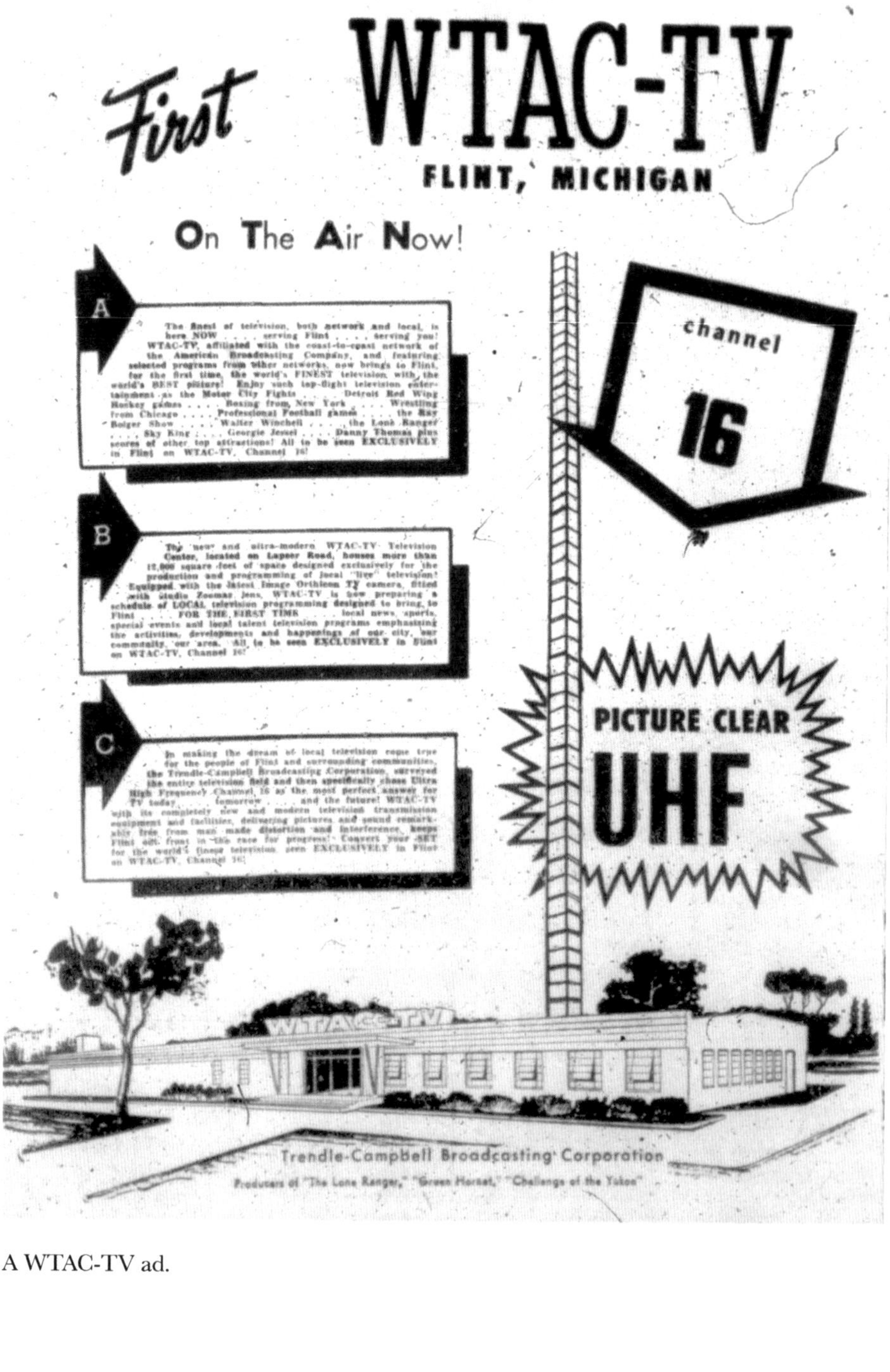
First
WTAC-TV
FLINT, MICHIGAN
On The Air Now!
A
The finest of television, both network and local, is here NOW . . . . serving Flint . . . . serving you! WTAC-TV, affiliated with the coast-to-coast network of the American Broadcasting Company, and featuring selected programs from other networks, now brings to Flint, for the first time, the world's FINEST television with the world's BEST picture! Enjoy such top-flight television entertainment as the Motor City Fights . . . . Detroit Red Wing Hockey games . . . . Boxing from New York . . . . Wrestling from Chicago . . . . Professional Football games . . . . the Ray Bolger Show . . . . Walter Winchell . . . . the Lone Ranger . . . . Sky King . . . . Georgie Jessel . . . . Danny Thomas plus scores of other top attractions! All to be seen EXCLUSIVELY in Flint on WTAC-TV, Channel 16!
B
The new and ultra-modern WTAC-TV Television Center, located on Lapeer Road, houses more than 12,000 square feet of space designed exclusively for the production and programming of local "live" television! Equipped with the latest Image Orthicon TV camera, fitted with Studio Zoomar lens, WTAC-TV is now preparing a schedule of LOCAL television programming designed to bring to Flint . . . FOR THE FIRST TIME . . . local news, sports, special events and local talent television programs emphasizing the activities, developments and happenings of our city, our community, our area. All to be seen EXCLUSIVELY in Flint on WTAC-TV, Channel 16!
C
In making the dream of local television come true for the people of Flint and surrounding communities, the Trendle-Campbell Broadcasting Corporation, surveyed the entire television field and then specifically chose Ultra High Frequency Channel 16 as the most perfect answer for TV today . . . tomorrow . . . and the future! WTAC-TV with its completely new and modern television transmission equipment and facilities, delivering pictures and sound remarkably free from man made distortion and interference, keeps Flint out front in the race for progress! Convert your SET for the world's finest television seen EXCLUSIVELY in Flint on WTAC-TV, Channel 16!
channel
16
PICTURE CLEAR
UHF
WTAC-TV
Trendle-Campbell Broadcasting Corporation
Producers of "The Lone Ranger," "Green Hornet," "Challenge of the Yukon"

A WTAC-TV ad.

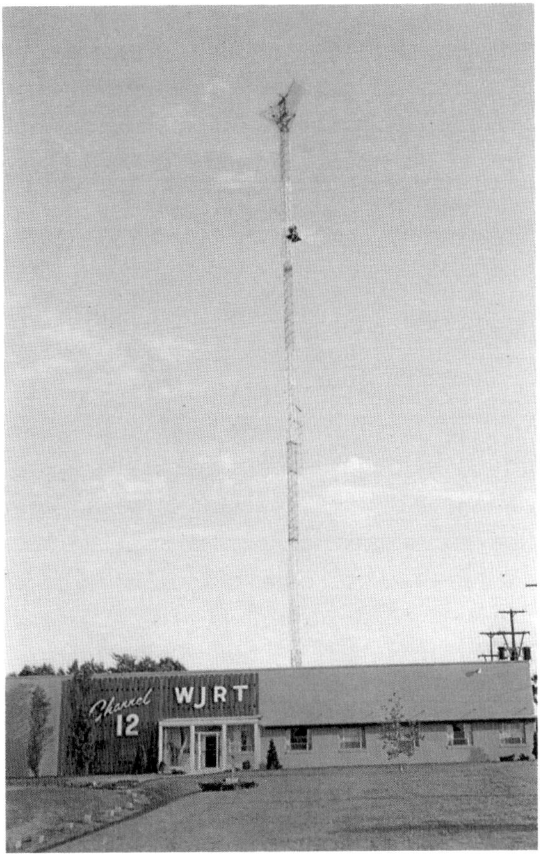

The WJRT (née WTAC-TV) studio as it originally looked.

Flint's television retailers were stocked heavily with TVs equipped with then-optional UHF TV tuners, as well as UHF converters, as most TVs at that time could only receive VHF channels 2 to 13. But it wasn't enough to sustain channel 16. Trendle-Campbell Broadcasting announced in April 1954 that it would suspend operation at month's end. Campbell said the shutdown "was forced upon us by a nationwide television condition and circumstances beyond our control." Indeed, most UHF TV stations at that time eventually shut down because most TVs back then were not equipped to receive UHF channels.

In August 1954, Trendle-Campbell surrendered the channel 16 operating license to the FCC, sold WTAC radio and transferred the lease of WTAC-TV's studios and offices to Goodwill Stations. Goodwill Stations was awarded the construction permit for the TV station on channel 12, which was granted the call letters WJRT. Goodwill received the permit upon appeal after the permit was originally granted to Trebit Corp.

More than four years of additional litigation would make Flint the largest American city without its own TV station. But Flint residents had plenty of TV options in the 1950s. Detroit stations WJBK-TV channel 2, WWJ-TV (now WDIV) channel 4 and WXYZ-TV channel 7 all boosted their signals in the 1950s so they could easily be received with outdoor antennas. WNEM-TV channel 5, an NBC primary affiliate and ABC secondary affiliate licensed to Bay City, signed on in February 1954 with the strongest signal in Flint at that time and maintained studios and offices at Bishop Airport.

Trebit Corp. proposed transmitting facilities about five miles north of Flint. Both Butterfield Theatres and Goodwill Stations proposed transmitting facilities in northern Oakland County—Butterfield Theatres near Holly and Goodwill Stations near Clarkston. Objections were raised by members of the Flint Citizens Committee for a VHF Television Station. They claimed that locating the transmitter in Oakland County would effectively make channel 12 a Detroit station rather than a Flint station because the signal would be received by more people in the Detroit area than in the Flint area.

Goodwill Stations decided in December 1954 to set up WJRT's transmitting facilities near Chesaning, a move that would give WJRT a strong signal, not only in Flint, but also in Saginaw, Bay City, Midland and Lansing. The Chesaning location led to objections raised by the owner of WKNX-TV channel 57, the CBS affiliate in Saginaw, claiming that the strong signal would force WKNX-TV out of business. WJRT's affiliation with the ABC television network muted that claim, as ABC had no primary affiliate in the cities served by the Chesaning transmitter. WJRT had unsuccessfully sought CBS affiliation before aligning with ABC. WJRT signed on for the first time, after a period of testing, on October 12, 1958, finally giving Flint its very own VHF TV signal.

THE REST OF THE STORY

In 1961, Congress passed the All-Channels Act, which authorized the FCC to require televisions sold in the United States to receive UHF channels effective for TVs manufactured on April 30, 1964. WKNX-TV managed to survive and moved to channel 25 in 1965. When WKNX-TV was sold in 1972, the call letters were changed to WEYI, and it moved its studios and offices from the Saginaw area to north of Clio on Willard Road. It had a 1,359-foot tower, the second-tallest structure in Michigan. With the new strong signal, CBS treated WEYI as Flint's CBS station, replacing WJIM-TV.

As for the vacant channel 16, the FCC changed the TV allocation table by the 1960s, replacing channel 16 with channel 66. A station was proposed with the calls WHAX-TV at that time, but it was never built. Channel 66 finally made it on air in 1985. WSMH was first an independent station and then a charter affiliate with the Fox Network in 1987.

In 1994, the National Football League made a deal with the Fox Network to carry NFC conference games instead of CBS, sparking a series of events that affected TV viewing habits around the country, including in Flint. First, New World Communications, the owner of Detroit CBS station WJBK at that time, switched all of its stations, including WJBK, to Fox. This left CBS scrambling to find new affiliates in the affected TV markets. One of the markets was Phoenix, Arizona. CBS signed with former independent KPHO, owned by Meredith Corporation. As part of the deal, CBS wanted and got co-owned and more desirable WNEM-TV in the Flint/Saginaw/Bay City TV market to switch from NBC to CBS. This forced NBC to find a new local affiliate. WSMH wanted to stay with Fox. ABC bought WJRT to keep that station as an ABC affiliate, leaving NBC with no choice but to affiliate with the old CBS station WEYI. The switch came at 3:00 a.m. on January 16, 1995. Only WEYI was on the air at that time, so at 2:59 a.m., then WEYI general manager Eric Land appeared live on camera to flip a symbolic knife switch with the CBS and NBC logos from CBS to NBC. He said, "The peacock has landed."

With the changeover to digital TV, Flint got digital TV allocations. WJRT initially was on digital channel 36. WFUM was on digital channel 52 but moved to 28 after shutting off its analog transmitter early. WSMH is on digital channel 16, the old WTAC-TV channel, but operates on virtual channel 66. The U.S. Congress mandated that the analog TV channels, including 12, 28 and 66 locally, be turned off permanently on February 17, 2009, but the date was moved to June 12, 2009. After the change, WJRT shifted its digital channel to channel 12. WJRT, in the old WTAC-TV studios and offices, is still there today, although in a much-expanded facility that Trendle and Campbell would not recognize.

In 2009, the University of Michigan announced that it would discontinue operations of WFUM channel 28, so it sold the PBS station to Central Michigan University, which took over in 2010. The call letters were changed to WCMZ-TV, with the station rebroadcasting the signal of WCMU-TV in Mt. Pleasant.

Update: The board of trustees of Central Michigan University, which operated Flint's PBS station WCMZ-TV channel 28, which rebroadcasts WCMU-TV in Mt. Pleasant, voted to sell the station's broadcast spectrum for $14 million. CMU bought what was then WFUM-TV from the University of Michigan for $1 million in 2009. The reason stated was that nearly all of channel 28's viewers can pick up other PBS stations, such as Delta College's WDCQ-TV channel 19 licensed to Bad Axe and Michigan State University's WKAR-TV channel 23 in East Lansing. CMU's other TV and radio stations would remain on the air. It did ask cable and satellite providers to keep CMU Public TV on their channel lineups. Channel 28 would go off the air by summer, allowing mobile and wireless devices to use the bandwidth.

The Citizens Bank Weather Ball

A Very Useful Landmark

Long before the Weather Channel existed and more than a decade before Flint even received cable TV, people in and around downtown Flint could look to the top of the Citizens Bank building and figure out the weather forecast each evening. Ever since the Citizens Bank weather ball was built in 1956, Flint residents and visitors who knew the weather ball rhyme knew what to expect:

When the weather ball is red,
Higher temperature's ahead.
When the weather ball is blue,
Lower temperature is due.
Yellow light in weather ball
Means there'll be no change at all.
When colors blink in agitation,
There's going to be precipitation.

The weather ball was built over a four-month period on top of the Citizens Bank headquarters. The headquarters were built in 1928 on the site of the original bank, which opened in 1871 at 328 South Saginaw Street. The weather ball has been the symbol of Citizens Bank ever since.

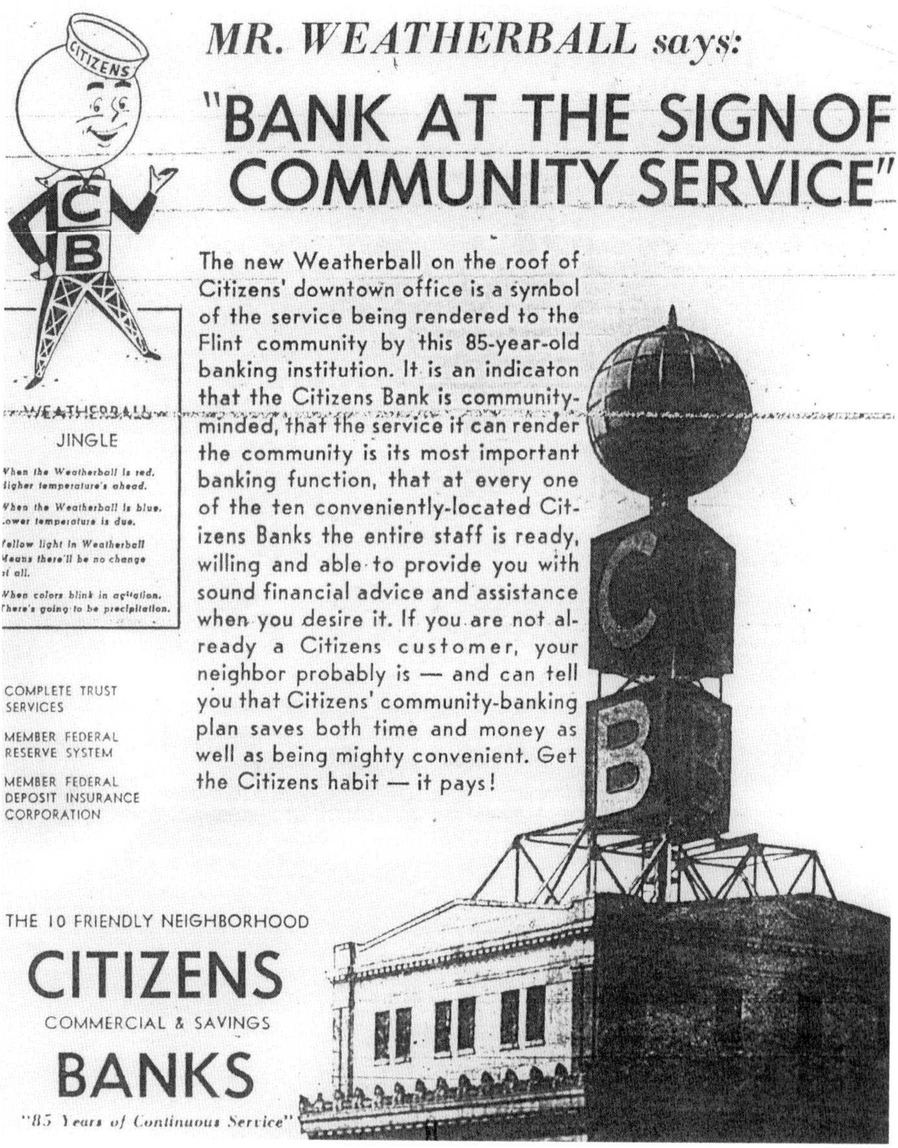

A 1956 advertisement introducing the weather ball.

The weather ball was first lit on the evening of October 30, 1956. Hundreds of balloons were released to mark the occasion. Three hundred of the balloons had Citizens Bank savings account credit cards inside.

Of course, the weather ball has become a symbol for Flint, just like the Statue of Liberty in New York, the Gateway Arch in St. Louis and the Eiffel Tower in Paris. When you see the weather ball, with the initials C.B. underneath, you know you are in Flint. The weather ball corporate symbol of Citizens Bank has changed over the years. My historic favorite is the mascot Mr. C.B. from the 1960s. (See "Flint's Cartoon Mascots" chapter.) In 2004, Citizens introduced its current corporate depiction of the weather ball—a red ball with white diagonal curved lines. Citizens' parent company, Citizens Republic Bancorp, is the largest bank holding company headquartered in Michigan. All other big banks in Michigan are headquartered out of state, including Comerica, which moved its headquarters from Detroit to Dallas, Texas, in 2007.

Thanks to Citizens Bank, here are some weather ball facts: The bank operates the weather ball and follows forecasts from the National Weather Service to determine which color the weather ball will be in the evening and whether it will blink or not. It was constructed by craftsmen from ten skilled trades using 800 square feet of Plexiglas and 667 feet of neon tubing. It weighs 2.5 tons, with a height and diameter of 15 feet and a circumference of 47 feet. It can be seen for 25 miles and is designed to withstand winds of up to 120 miles per hour.

During the 1970s energy crisis, the weather ball was turned off from 1974 to January 1978 to save electricity. It was briefly lit for a few days in 1977 to make sure everything was working properly. Some neon work was needed to get the weather ball fully functioning again. There are or were other weather balls constructed by banks, such as the ones built by Michigan National Bank in Grand Rapids, the Texas National Bank in Houston and Northwestern Bank in Minneapolis, along with KCAU-TV in Sioux City, Iowa. Grand Rapids TV station WZZM channel 13 bought the dismantled Michigan National Bank weather ball, restored it and moved it to its studio location at the I-96 and U.S. 131 interchange.

The inside of the weather ball has to be an impressive sight, with its alternating red, blue and yellow neon tubing. About 2002, it received new breaker panels, transformers and wiring. For its fiftieth anniversary in 2006, Citizens hired three local companies to completely refurbish the weather ball, including an inside-and-out power washing, new paint, new wiring, new electrical connections and, where necessary, new neon tubing. Citizens Bank contracts with Signs by Crannie for new signs and maintenance of existing signs, including the weather ball. The Citizens Bank weather ball continues to be a prominent feature of downtown Flint's skyline and serves as a giant eyeball watching over the city.

Thanks to Citizens Bank.

Update: After FirstMerit Bank took over Citizens Bank, the neon *CB* letters were taken down and the letters *FM*, along with its diamond-shaped logo, were put up below the weather ball. The Huntington National Bank, which bought FirstMerit in August 2016, has stated that it will keep the weather ball. There have been calls for Huntington to install the new letters in the same style as the scrapped *CB* letters. How the weather ball would look after Huntington converted the FirstMerit branches to Huntington branches on February 21, 2017, was not revealed by the deadline for this book.

The Bookstore Raids of October 1963

Let's go back to a more innocent time, before the 1960s became turbulent. It's the fall of 1963, shortly before we lost that innocence when President Kennedy was assassinated on November 22. The lead figure in this tale is Genesee County's young and ambitious prosecutor, Robert F. Leonard.

Leonard organized a citizen's committee to help rid Genesee County newsstands of "obscene and pornographic" literature. Today, of course, adults can access the Internet or go into the "eighteen or over" closets in video stores to see porn that is much more graphic than what Leonard was going after.

The work Leonard led bore fruit on October 9, when Flint police detectives and members of Leonard's staff raided four bookstores and arrested two bookstore owners and an employee. A fourth person was arrested the following day. The bookstores raided were the downtown Le Stag Shoppe at 310 South Saginaw, Readmore Newstand at 730 North Saginaw and the Book Nook at 203 North Saginaw and Book-Mark at 3308 Corunna on the west side of town.

Several boxes of magazines and books that Leonard said were obscene were confiscated. The stores were padlocked to allow members of his staff to examine the books and magazines inside. Titles Leonard mentioned included *Fabulous Femmes*, *Lace Undies*, *Caper*, *Dynamic Nudist*, *Nudist Colorama*, *Gentleman*, *Ace*, *Black Satin*, *Gent*, *Swank*, *Modern Man*, *Big Show*, *Heat Wave*, *Art*

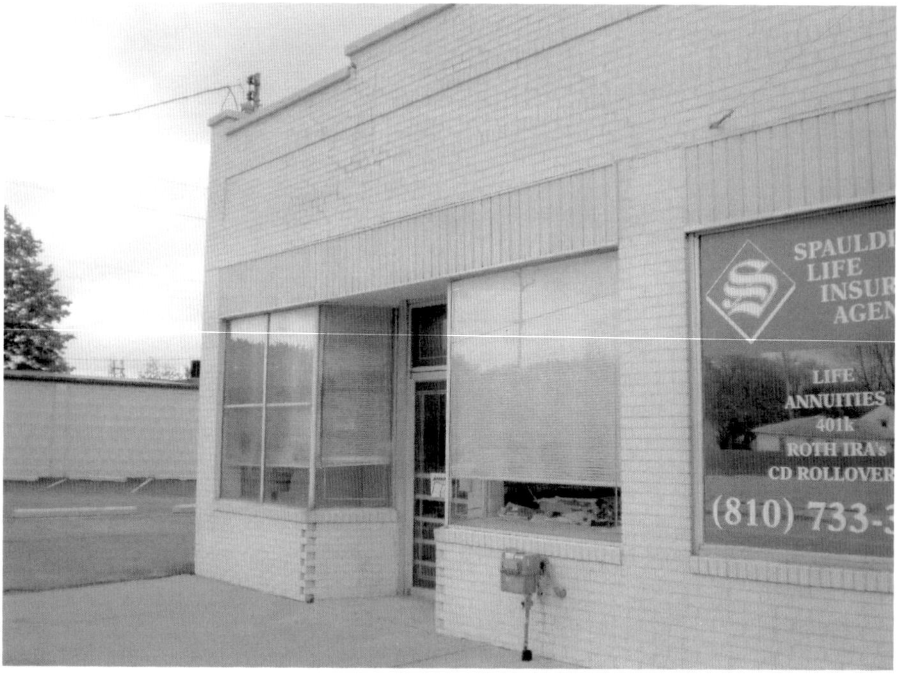

The former Book-Mark location on Corunna Road, the last former bookstore standing.

Films, *High Heels*, *Honey*, *Cloud-9*, *Feline*, *Sun Era*, *Satana* and *Nite'ee*. The listed magazine titles showed that what was called pornography by Leonard in 1963 was mild and could be considered soft porn today; they are mainly girlie or nudist magazines.

The charges were circuit court misdemeanors with a maximum penalty of a $1,000 fine and one year in jail. The padlocks were removed on October 12. One month later, municipal judge Basil Baker granted a petition by the American Civil Liberties Union (ACLU) to act as a friend of the court. The petition was filed by attorneys Harry Newblatt and Marvin Failer. Newblatt and Failer acted on behalf of the Book Nook's operator.

The first defendant in court pleaded guilty to the charge of lending an obscene motion picture on October 28. He was an employee of Le Stag and had lent the film to an undercover agent for a fee. On December 10, he was put on one year's probation by Judge Stewart A. Newblatt.

The trials for the three remaining defendants took place the following April. Leonard suffered a setback on April 9, when Judge Donn D. Parker

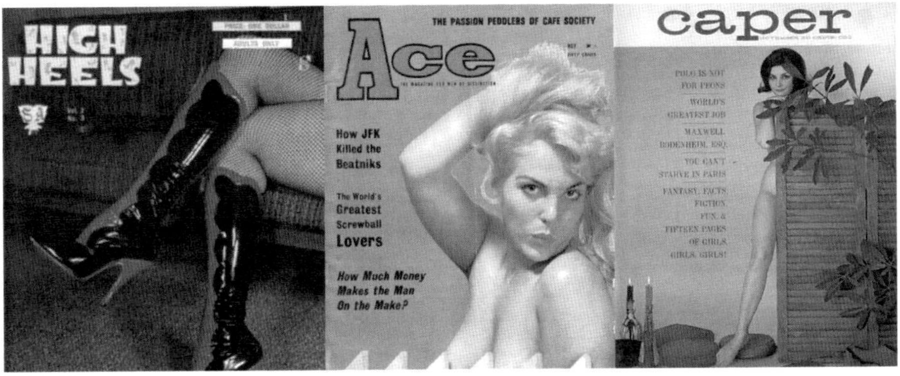

Examples of magazines seized in the bookstore raid.

criticized the prosecutor's office and law enforcement officials for padlocking one of the bookstores, as the contents were not obscene in his opinion but were instead "coarse and vulgar." Judge Parker dismissed the charges against the owner of Le Stag Shoppe. The seized merchandise was ordered returned. Leonard decided to try a new line of attack, concentrating on films and paperback books rather than magazines.

Leonard suffered another setback when Judge Stewart Newblatt dismissed the charge against the owner of Book-Mark, agreeing with Judge Parker about the earlier dismissal. Judge Stewart Newblatt was Harry Newblatt's brother, so a defense attorney from Detroit, Ernest Goodman, was brought in. Judge Newblatt granted two motions by Goodman, one stating that the magazines were seized illegally and could not be used and the other asking for dismissal of the charge. Judge Newblatt also quashed the search warrant and ordered the seized magazines returned.

The charge against the Book Nook operator was dismissed on April 27 by Judge John W. Baker, who ruled that the search warrant for the Book Nook raid was invalid and the publications seized there did not violate state law. The merchandise was ordered returned to the Book Nook's operator. Judge Baker concurred with the other judges that the publications were "coarse and vulgar" but not obscene.

As for what became of the bookstores, Le Stag and Book Nook did not survive 1964, although the Le Stag location in the Sunlin Building where the Royal Theatre (which showed adult movies) was located housed other adult bookstores until it was torn down in 1973 to make way for an addition to

Citizens Bank. The Book-Mark on Corunna Road became Front Page Book Center in 1979 before it closed; the address was occupied by a bakery in 1983. Today, that location is a dusty little used office next to a life insurance agency. It is the only former bookstore building still standing. Readmore, the only bookstore not prosecuted, also lasted several years, moving into a nearby larger location at 714 North Saginaw in 1972. It became a Front Page book center in 1981. It was forced to close to make way for the ill-fated AutoWorld in 1982.

Marvin Failer was with the law firm of Bueche, Failer, O'Callaghan & Zintsmaster in Flushing until he retired. Harry P. Newblatt was elected district court judge for the newly formed Flushing District Court in 1968. Judge Harry Newblatt acquired the nickname of "Hurry-up Harry" because of his reputation in keeping the court moving along to deal with his caseload. He was reelected in 1972, 1978 and 1984 before retiring from the bench in 1989. He died on April 10, 2002, at age seventy-six. As for prosecutor Robert Leonard, he unsuccessfully ran for circuit court judge in 1966. Despite the setbacks, he had success as county prosecutor, bringing him national attention with his innovative ideas to improve justice and reduce court backlogs. He also set up consumer protection and white-collar crime programs that were copied elsewhere. His downfall was with managing public funds. A fund set up to pay informants of organized crime and drug dealing had $34,000 missing, and a federal grand jury indicted him. He was convicted in 1979 of tax evasion and embezzlement (thus stripped of his job as county prosecutor) and was sentenced, in 1980, to five years in prison and fined $15,000. He was released after serving forty-four months in a federal penitentiary. Admitting that he made mistakes, Leonard attempted a political comeback in 1987, when he ran for Fifth Ward city councilman, but he lost to incumbent councilman Matt Taylor.

The Dort Mall

Magnet for Collectible Buffs

A once-glorious shopping center that was considered *the* place to shop back in the 1960s is still a great place to stop and shop thanks to its owner's vast collection of collectible items. The Dort Mall was the Flint area's first enclosed shopping mall and was built in two stages in 1964 and '65. In the first phase, the Yankee Stadium store, now the south part of the mall, was built. The rest of the mall, anchored at the time by an A&P supermarket, was completed in 1965. A movie theater addition was added in 1968. The Dort Mall was built by William Oleksyn on the site of his Dort Drive-In Theatre. That mall would be overtaken in the 1970s by the Eastland Mall (now Courtland Center) and Genesee Valley Center.

By the mid-1970s, the bulk of its original tenants had moved out. The Yankee store, renamed Zodys, closed in 1975. A&P had also closed by that time. In 1976, the mall was renovated and renamed the Small Mall. The former Yankee Stadium Store was subdivided. A Sears Surplus store took over much of the Yankee store space, along with a bingo hall and smaller shops. Circus Time Pizza occupied the former A&P store. Circus Time was a combination pizza parlor and video arcade similar to Chuck E. Cheese, with robotic entertainers on stage. A nightclub/disco called The Light operated in the mall's basement. The mall continued to struggle and went through three different owners in the 1980s and 1990s. The cinema (split into a two-screen theater in 1975) closed in 1983. The owner of the Court

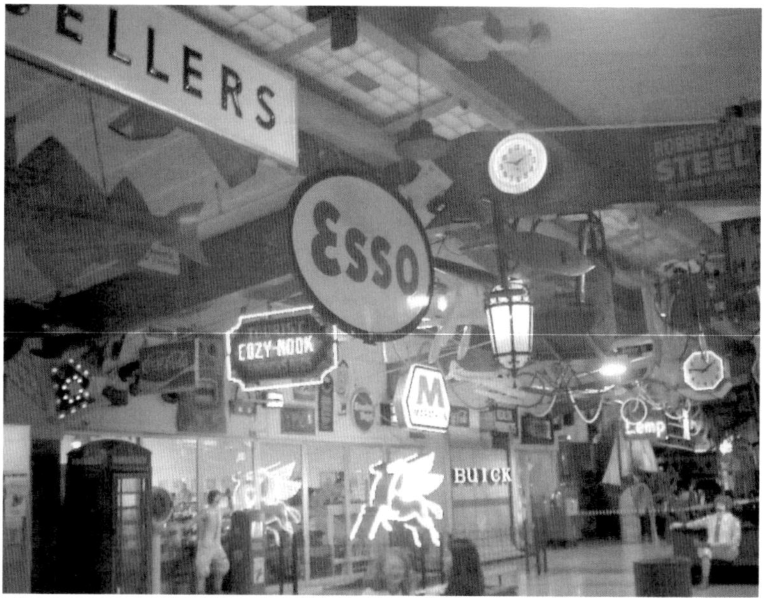

A 2005 photo of the Dort Mall collection.

Theatre in Saginaw showed interest in leasing the twin theater but decided not to because he realized it could not compete with the then-dominant Showcase Cinemas on East Court Street (now closed). General Cinemas, which leased the theater, stripped it of equipment and fixtures before the lease expired. The Small Mall was renamed the Mid-America Plaza in 1984. The mall management installed speed bumps in the parking lot because it had become a magnet for cruisers. Sears Surplus, The Light and Circus Time Pizza did not survive the 1980s. Before Circus Time went bankrupt, it tried live entertainment with well-known stand-up comedians as Circus Time After Dark.

In 1995, businessman James Patton sold the mall to businessman and local hockey legend Bob Perani, a former minor-league goalie who was a member of the original Flint Generals. After acquiring the mall, Perani's Hockey Shop moved into the mall to become one of the anchor stores. The other anchor stores in the mall are Bargain Hunterz and Big Lots. Probably the longest-operating tenant in the mall is Star Brothers Coney Island, which opened in the former Walgreens restaurant in the 1970s. About a third of the mall's space at its north end was converted from retail space to office space. The former cinema became a maintenance office and storage area. Perani restored the original Dort Mall name.

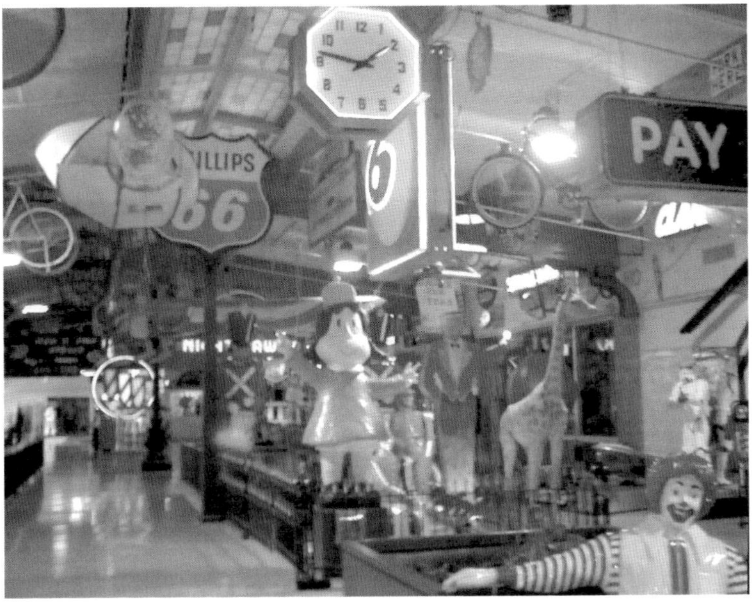

A 2005 photo of additional items in the Dort Mall collection.

But what makes the Dort Mall interesting nowadays is Perani's vast collection of antiques, old neon signs, gasoline pumps, gas station signs, movie props, promotional castoffs, deep sea–diving suits, old ship figureheads, boats, public scales, vintage traffic signs, two red British phone booths and other collectibles that included two single-engine airplanes and a merry-go-round in 2005. Outside, you can see old ship anchors, airplane propellers, the old Walli's West Restaurant revolving neon star and a huge statue of *Mad* magazine mascot Alfred E. Neuman.

Perani admits to having been a junk collector and nautical buff all his life. He acquired most of his collection through auctions around the country. He auctioned off a third of his own collection in the mall in 2003 and again in 2009 to make room for more items. The movie props include two model ships: a Roman galley used in the 1959 movie *Ben Hur* and the ship the *Flounder*, which Dr. Doolittle, played by Rex Harrison, sailed in the 1967 film *Doctor Doolittle*. In front of these prop ships are two ancient cannons from the early 1700s. One was a Patterero cannon that Perani found in Florida, and the other was a Spanish cannon from a sunken ship in the Atlantic. The collection is so vast that you could visit the mall many times and note something new each time. How did the two airplanes get inside the mall? The wings could easily have been removed and reassembled. One of the two planes was actually made in Flint. It was an Ace Aircraft made by the Ace Aircraft Company, in business from 1929 to 1932.

One historical item of note in 2005 was the Otisville "drunk tank," a jail cell that was in the basement of the Otisville Village Hall from 1910 to the 1940s and housed Saturday night drunks. Of all the gas station signs in the mall, Perani was most proud of the two-sided neon Mobil Oil Pegasus sign, one of only a half dozen two-sided neon Mobil Pegasus signs known to be in existence. Most of the electric signs in the mall are in working order because Perani contracts with a neon sign repairman to restore the signs in his collection. In front of Perani's Hockey Shop is a restored 1960s vintage Zamboni used to resurface ice at hockey arenas and a late 1800s vintage church bell from a Catholic church in Albany, New York, made by the Meneely Bell Company of Troy, New York.

Flint's Buick heritage is represented by old car show mementoes, including Buick signs and a displayed 1996 vintage 3800 Series II 3.8 liter V-6 engine standard in LeSabre, Park Avenue and Rivera models and optional on the Regal. That engine was made at the GM Powertrain Flint North engine plant, which closed in 2008.

Standing tall in the mall before the 2009 auction were an old four-sided post clock from a small Georgia town and a Phillips 66 sign. Statues inside the mall included two Ronald McDonalds, one sitting on a bench and one in a standing pose; Little Lulu; and two wooden soldiers from a J.L. Hudson Thanksgiving Parade in Detroit. Many more items are stored in vacant mall spaces.

The collection continues to evolve and change, so I suggest doing some of your shopping at the Dort Mall at the corner of South Dort Highway and Atherton Road in Flint. Admire the collection while you're there.

Thanks to Bob Perani.

Update: After mall owner Bob Perani died in 2012, the Perani family sold off most of the collectibles inside and outside the Dort Mall, where Perani's Hockey World is still based.

Remembering Local Rock Legend Terry Knight

On November 1, 2004, Flint-area music icon Terry Knight was stabbed to death by his daughter's boyfriend in an apartment they shared in Temple, Texas. Terry Knight was a radio disc jockey in the 1960s. He fronted his own locally popular rock group, Terry Knight & the Pack, which he later reorganized and managed into the most successful musical act to originate from Flint: Grand Funk Railroad. It was a sad and tragic end to a man who led a colorful life.

One notable local shrine to Grand Funk is an old railroad viaduct on Fenton Road, south of Twelfth Street. The viaduct isn't much to look at, but in the 1970s it became a makeshift shrine to Grand Funk. The painted sign on the viaduct originally read "Grand Trunk Western RR," but someone painted over the "TR" in "trunk" and substituted the letter "F" in its place, so "Grand Trunk" read "Grand Funk." Shortly after Knight's death, a wreath with a checkered flag was hung on the viaduct.

Terry Knight was born Richard Terrance Knapp in Lapeer on April 9, 1943. He became a radio deejay as a teenager, using the on-air name Terry Knight in the early 1960s. He would later legally change his surname from Knapp to Knight. After he became popular on Flint radio stations WTRX, WTAC and WAMM, he went to the Windsor/Detroit powerhouse radio station CKLW. His musical ambitions got the best of him, and he quit radio to try his hand at performing. He got together with a Flint-based group

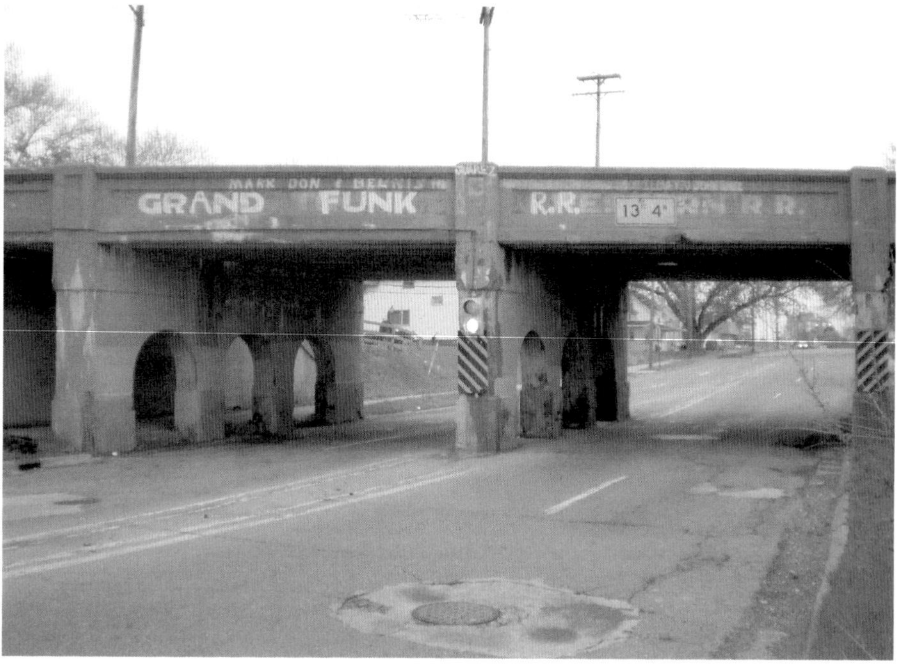

The Grand Funk shrine at the CN (former Grand Trunk) Fenton Road viaduct.

called the Jazz Masters, whose members included Mark Farner and Don Brewer, and the group became Terry Knight & the Pack. This group would have a string of regional hits, beginning in 1966 with a fine cover version of the Yardbirds' hit "Better Man Than I." The group's biggest hit was a cover of Ben E. King's "I Who Have Nothing," which made it to number forty-six nationally. Terry Knight left the Pack to try his hand as a solo artist. When that didn't pan out, he reorganized the Pack into Grand Funk Railroad in 1969 with lead guitarist Farner and drummer Brewer, who were joined by bass guitarist Mel Schacher. Of course, the name Grand Funk Railroad was inspired by the Grand Trunk Railroad (now absorbed into Canadian National [CN]), which runs through Flint.

Knight retired from performing to become Grand Funk's manager. Grand Funk would become one of the most successful rock groups of the 1970s. But the band and Knight had a falling out, and Knight was fired by the group in 1972, sparking a legal battle in which Knight received a multimillion-dollar settlement. After unsuccessfully promoting other musical acts, he quit the music business and maintained a low profile. He did invest in a Grand Prix racing venture with actor Paul Newman, a move that may explain the checkered flag on the wreath, but he squandered his fortune on an expensive lifestyle that included cocaine addiction. He settled into a nomadic existence, and it was rumored that he was in the witness protection program. A strange and sad life, indeed, and it ended in a Temple, Texas apartment, where he lived off his Grand Funk royalties.

Terry Knight embodied—indeed, shaped—the spirit, work ethic and take-no-prisoners approach to making dreams reality and life an adventure that this area holds dear. For that, and more, he will be greatly missed. His cremated remains were buried in the Knapp family plot at Mount Hope Cemetery in Lapeer.

Keith Moon's Infamous Birthday Party in Flint

On August 23, 1967, one of the most significant events in Flint music history occurred, although it was not widely reported at that time. It began with a matinee rock concert at Atwood Stadium headlined by Herman's Hermits, with opening acts the Blues Magoos and, more significantly, The Who. The concert date also marked Who drummer Keith Moon's twenty-first birthday.

The Who's first hit, "I Can't Explain," was first played in the United States in Flint on WTAC (now WSNL) and WTRX in December 1964. It became a big regional hit while just cracking the national charts at number ninety-seven in early 1965. According to a Decca Records ad for the song in the February 13, 1965 issue of *Billboard* magazine, the song was also a breakout in Detroit, Pontiac, Lansing and Toledo. The local success of this and subsequent Who records led to Flint becoming a tour stop for The Who. WTAC's Peter C. Cavanaugh recalled the events of that afternoon and evening in 1967 in his book, *Local DJ*. After the Blues Magoos finished their thirty-minute set with their big hit, "We Ain't Got Nothin' Yet," The Who came on after setting up for twenty minutes.

The Who literally exploded on the Atwood Stadium platform with their eardrum-shattering set, flaming guitar playing and instrument-smashing finale, which left the stage completely destroyed, just like when they performed the month before at the Monterey Pop Festival. The headliner, Herman's

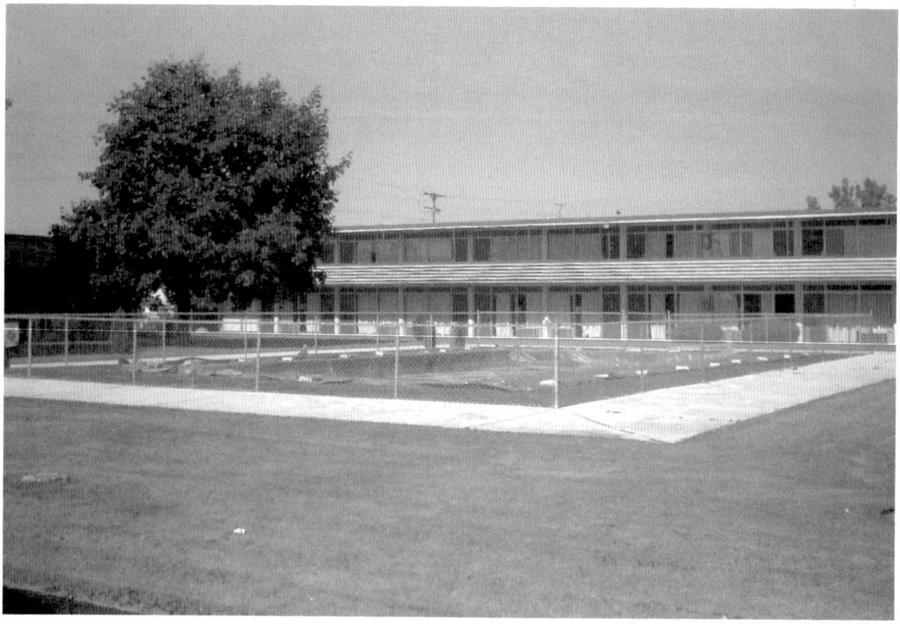

The former Holiday Inn (then Days Inn) swimming pool in 2007.

Hermits, was aghast at having to sing an old British music hall song—"I'm Henry the Eighth, I Am," a number one American hit for them—after that destructive performance. Still pumped up after the show, The Who trashed what was left of their dressing room, and Keith Moon kicked a field goal with a wastebasket from fifty feet away. A national audience would see a similarly explosive show a month later when The Who performed on *The Smothers Brothers Comedy Hour* on CBS television.

After the show, a birthday party for Keith was held at the Holiday Inn on Bristol Road near Bishop Airport. Decca Records made the arrangements for the party in the inn's largest conference room. The festivities included a huge birthday cake, provided by Premier Drums, with a half-naked young woman popping out of the cake. The bar was open, and everyone got intoxicated. A food fight developed involving pieces of the cake.

At this point, there are many interpretations of what happened at the Holiday Inn. The inn's manager complained about the noise. Fire extinguishers were set off, and the foam was sprayed on guests' cars, ruining the finishes. A piano was reduced to kindling. Keith broke a tooth when he tripped on a piece of cake while trying to run away from a sheriff's deputy. The carpeting needed replacing.

What the stories about the event do not agree on is whether Keith drove a luxury car into the Holiday Inn pool. Author Tony Fletcher, in his biography of Keith Moon, debunks the myth that Keith drove a Rolls-Royce into the pool. No one in Flint would believe that claim anyway. I was convinced that it was a Lincoln Continental, as Keith himself stated in an interview for *Rolling Stone* magazine. Peter C. Cavanaugh wrote that it was a Cadillac. Whatever the case, the total bill, including damages incurred, was $24,000. It was rumored that Decca Records purchased the damp Cadillac from its irate owner.

Depending on which story you believe, either Genesee County sheriff Thomas Bell or one of Herman's Hermits sent Keith to a local dentist, who had to be awakened to repair the rock star's tooth before he was sent to the county jail to spend the night. The story goes that Keith was so drunk that no Novocain was needed. A charter plane had to be brought in to take Keith to the next tour stop in Philadelphia. While taking him to the plane, Sheriff Bell told Keith, "Son, don't ever dock in Flint, Michigan, again." It was boasted that the group was banned from all Holiday Inns worldwide. The ban against The Who was ceremoniously lifted by Holiday Inn during a 1999 VH-1 special about Keith Moon's twenty-first birthday party.

Even with The Who's and Herman's Hermits' offstage performances at the Holiday Inn outdoing the onstage performances at Atwood Stadium, neither performance was reported in the *Flint Journal* at that time.

In 1985, the Holiday Inn at 2207 West Bristol Road was sold and converted into a Days Inn. The Holiday Inn neon sign was in place until the conversion. The pool is still there. In 2007, the two-story west building in the complex, which was the Airport Inn, was completely renovated and became a Rodeway Inn at 2215 West Bristol Road. In 2010, both motels were closed and completely fenced in. All motel signs were removed.

No matter how the events that took place on Keith Moon's twenty-first birthday are interpreted, it is agreed that the birthday party cemented Keith's reputation as a hotel wrecker. Keith Moon died on September 7, 1978, of a drug overdose at age thirty-two. His ashes are at the Golders Green Crematorium in London, England.

See Peter C. Cavanaugh's Local DJ: A Rock 'n' Roll History *(2002) and* The Rolling Stone Interviews, 1967–1980 *(1989), by the editors of* Rolling Stone, *for more information.*

Flint's Connection with *The Gong Show*

This story is about how a Flint radio station broke one of the biggest hits of 1962: "Palisades Park," performed by Freddy Cannon and composed by Chuck Barris. Yes, *that* Chuck Barris.

By the end of the 1950s, the practice of record companies paying radio station disc jockeys to play certain records had come under legal scrutiny. Called "payola," the practice was made illegal in the United States in 1960. Some radio station disc jockeys—most notably Alan Freed, who coined the term "rock and roll"—found themselves in serious legal trouble from payola and their radio careers suddenly ended. One of the most notable disc jockeys was Dick Clark, who hosted the nationally broadcast TV series *American Bandstand* from Philadelphia on ABC. Clark had a financial interest in record and music publishing companies, but because of the payola scandal, ABC forced Clark to divest himself of his music holdings if he wanted to continue as host of *American Bandstand.*

To keep watch over Dick Clark, ABC hired a young broadcasting executive who was recently laid off from NBC. This young upstart was named Chuck Barris. Barris had access to everyone on *American Bandstand*, as well as to all aspects of production. Everyone was distrustful of the outsider from ABC, except for Clark. Barris made copious notes about all aspects of the show's production. The final report Barris submitted to ABC was a five-hundred-page compilation of his memos, which were turned over to a House congressional committee investigating payola. The committee cleared Clark of any wrongdoing, resulting in a close friendship between Clark and Barris.

While in Philadelphia, Barris spent his free time writing songs. One of those songs was given to frequent *American Bandstand* guest Freddy Cannon. After Barris's work on *American Bandstand* was done, he was made a junior executive in ABC's daytime programming department. Meanwhile, Cannon decided to record Barris's song as the B-side of a song Cannon co-wrote called "June, July and August" in 1962.

Flint's top forty radio station, WTAC "WeeTac Big 600" (now religious station WSNL), put "June, July and August" on its playlist. But one day, a WTAC deejay accidently played the B-side to that song. What WTAC played instead was "Palisades Park," and the phones lit up. Listeners wanted to hear the song again. Former WTAC deejay Pete Flanders said that Cannon (who frequently performed in Flint) claimed that Bob Dell (real name Bob DelGiorno) was the deejay who first played that song. But when DelGiorno (now in Louisiana) was contacted, he replied that he was working at WOLF in Syracuse, New York, at the time "Palisades Park" broke and didn't join WTAC until the fall of 1963. Local radio veteran Marty Natchez believes that WTAC's midday deejay at that time, the late Ed Berryman, first played the song. Cannon's label, Swan Records, contacted other radio stations and asked them to flip the record over. The song became a huge hit, reaching number three on the charts. It became an international hit as well.

The hit earned Barris $30,000 in royalties in 1962. But when "Palisades Park" hit, the ABC bosses gave the budding songwriter an ultimatum, forcing him to chose between TV programming and songwriting. They feared another payola investigation. Barris stuck with TV programming.

Barris was transferred to Los Angeles and put in charge of choosing which game show concepts ABC should buy and put on the air. He complained to his bosses that the shows being pitched to him were worse than his own ideas. So the bosses suggested that he quit his programming job and become a producer himself.

Barris borrowed $20,000 from his stepfather to produce a pilot for his first show, *The Dating Game*, in 1965. ABC turned down the show, a move that depressed the now self-employed but broke Barris. A month later, the shows ABC aired instead flopped in the ratings. So ABC dusted off Barris's pilot and bought *The Dating Game*. The success of that show led ABC to ask him for another show. *The Newlywed Game* made its debut in 1966. The host of

The Newlywed Game, Bob Eubanks, was born in Flint and was a disc jockey for a Los Angeles radio station at that time. *The Newlywed Game* was a hit as well. Barris came up with additional shows, but none of these late 1960s shows had the staying power of *The Dating Game* and *The Newlywed Game*.

In 1975, Barris and TV variety show producer Chris Bearde collaborated on a new show concept. The idea was a parody of talent shows; they would intentionally present bad acts as well as good acts. Borrowing an idea from old-time radio's *Major Bowes' Amateur Hour*, if any judge on the show's panel thought an act was bad, the judge would bang a gong, and the act would immediately stop. That idea was sold to ABC for its owned-and-operated stations, and the weekly prime time access syndicated version of *The Gong Show* with Gary Owens debuted on local stations in September 1976. Meanwhile, Barris sold NBC a daytime network version of that show. A week's worth of shows were taped with host John Barbour. But Barbour didn't get the concept of the show as satire and treated it as a straight talent show. An NBC executive noticed the problem and, after seeing Barris himself consoling the gonged acts, decided that either Barris would host the show or NBC would not buy the series.

The daytime show made its debut on June 14, 1976. It became an immediate hit, and Barris became a reluctant star. The show became even wilder as time progressed, with ongoing acts such as the Unknown Comic (comedian Murray Langston) and Gene Gene the Dancing Machine (NBC stagehand Gene Patton). Later episodes showed a Flint Generals hockey team pennant over the gong. When Gary Owens's hosting contract expired, Barris took over the nighttime show as well. Chris Bearde was also let go but would still get paid as a *Gong Show* co-creator. *The Gong Show* pushed the envelope over what would pass the network censors, and a few of the most tasteless acts did get edited from the show. But one act in 1978 managed to slip through the NBC censors. It was called Have You Got a Nickel, better known as the Popsicle Twins—two teenage girls whose act was suggestively sucking on popsicles. The phones lit up on the East Coast, and the girls' segment was edited out of the West Coast feed. *The Gong Show* crossed the line, and NBC canceled the show. The final NBC broadcast aired on July 21, 1978.

The show continued in syndication, and Barris introduced two other short-lived game shows. *The $1.98 Beauty Show* was a parody of beauty pageants that had as one contestant future comedy star and Flint native

Sandra Bernhard. She won. *Three's a Crowd* had three man/wife/secretary teams of contestants in a *Newlywed Game* format; it was so controversial that, in 1980, a burned-out Barris shut down production of all his shows. *Gong Show* reruns are occasionally aired on the GSN cable channel, and segments (including the Popsicle Twins) can be found online on YouTube. As a pioneer of reality TV, you can see echoes of *The Gong Show* on *American Idol.* Barris sold his production company in 1986; it is now owned by Sony Pictures Television. But we may not have enjoyed these guilty pleasures if it wasn't for WTAC playing "Palisades Park" by mistake.

Inspired by a documentary about Chuck Barris produced by GSN, The Chuck Barris Story: My Life on the Edge, *aired in 2006.*

A Visit to a Sign Company's Boneyard

When a business closes and a new occupant occupies an address, the sign gets changed from the old business to the new business. Mergers and acquisitions also lead to sign changes. When a business adopts a new logo, the sign is changed accordingly. What happens to the old sign? The sign company that changed the signs usually places the old sign in its "boneyard."

The term is sometimes a misnomer because signs for national or regional chains are often stored in the boneyard before they are needed for a new location. Also, seasonal businesses that often move from year to year store their signs in the boneyard during the off-season.

For this visit, *Uncommon Sense* photographer Harry Awdey and myself went to Signs by Crannie in 2006. It is a bustling local sign company that designs, fabricates, installs and maintains different varieties of signs for businesses. The company makes signs not just for local businesses but also for national clients. Dan Crannie mentioned new signs that the company made in 2006 for shipment to Indianapolis. T.J. was our tour guide.

The first notable sign for a defunct business I noticed was for a restaurant I used to eat in. Saltmarsh Annie's was a seafood and steak restaurant at 2324 South Ballenger Highway near Miller Road, where Liu's Buffet (since closed) was later located. There have been several businesses at that building over the years. It was originally a Ponderosa steakhouse in 1969.

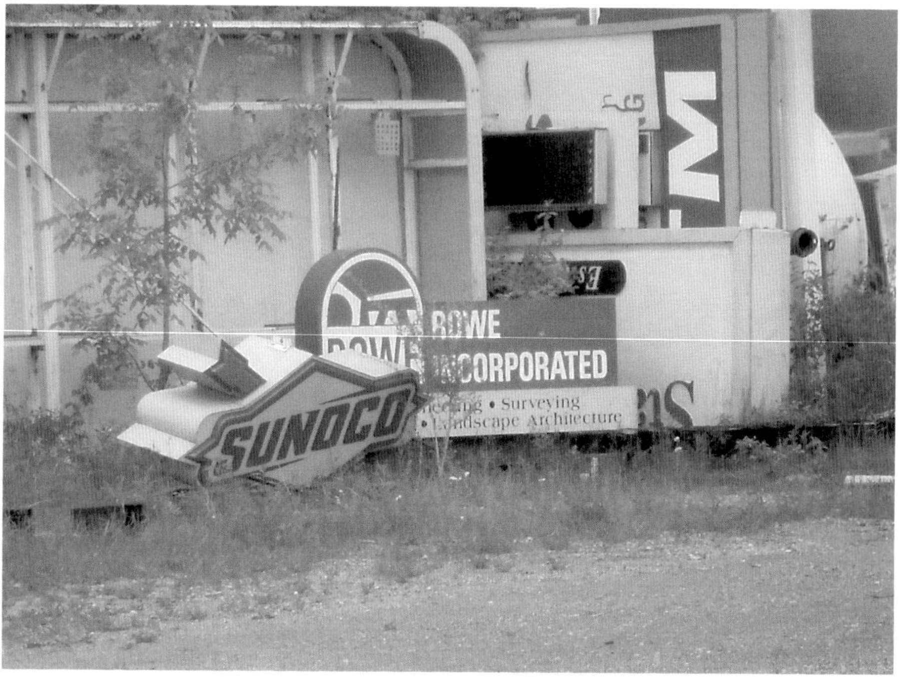

A Rowe Inc. sign among those in the boneyard.

Ponderosa closed about 1987, and the building was vacant until it was renovated and became a Total Video store in 1990. After Total Video closed in 1996, it was renovated and became a restaurant again, Laredo Steakhouse, in 1997. This restaurant was noted for having a flagpole in front with the flag of Texas flying. In 2000, the restaurant was remodeled and became Saltmarsh Annie's. In 2005, the restaurant was remodeled again and became Liu's Buffet Chinese restaurant. In 2010, it was closed and put up for sale.

But I'm digressing. I found another sign I recall from days gone by: Garrison's Hardware. It was located where a Pennzoil 10 Minute Oil Change shop is now at 1114 South Ballenger Highway and Corunna Road. Garrison's is still around as a trailer hitch shop and rent-all store nearby, at 4108 Corunna Road. CVS Pharmacy once had several locations in the Flint area, but the company decided to pull out of the area, so the nearest CVS location is in Holly nowadays. Borders, the big-box bookstore chain, experimented with an outlet store for remaindered books in a Linden Road

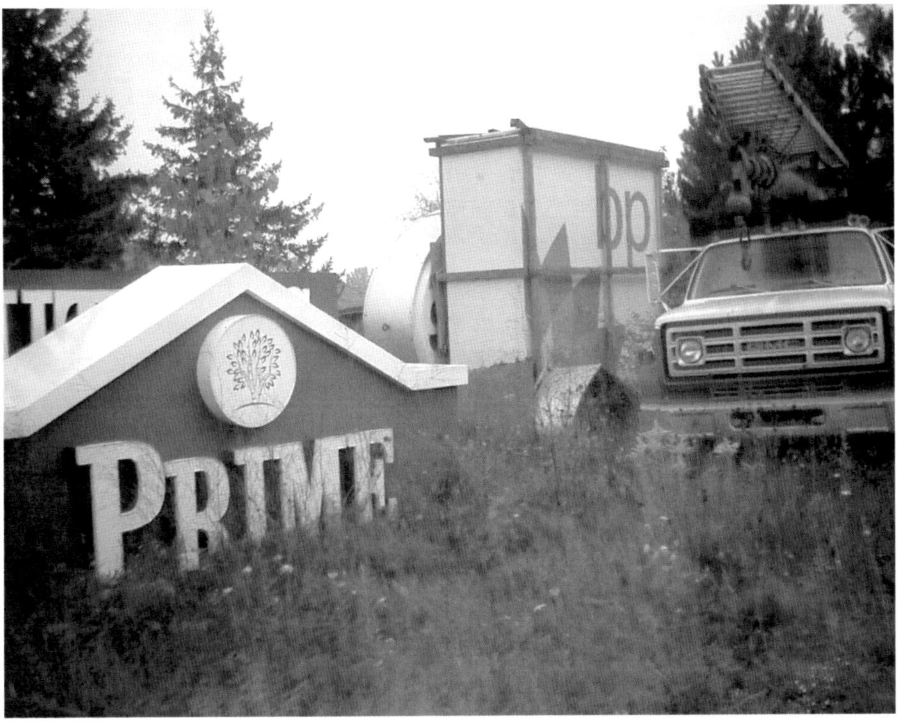

A retired Prime Outlets sign.

strip mall but decided to close it. So the Borders Outlet letters were also in the boneyard. Front Row Video was a high-end TV and stereo shop associated with Stereo Center, which was also on Linden Road. Stereo Center moved to the Ross Plaza on Miller Road after Front Row Video closed, but it folded. The Stereo Center sign originally on Linden Road was still above the former Miller Road location for a while before it was taken down to make way for a new tenant.

One major job Signs by Crannie undertook beginning in 2003 was to change all the signs on the local Amoco gas stations to BP stations. BP merged with Amoco in 1998 and began the phase-in from Amoco/Standard to BP in 2000. So all the familiar Amoco and Standard torch and oval signs officially disappeared from the gas stations in 2004. Some wound up in the hands of sign collectors, as old gas station signs are quite collectable. You can still see Amoco signs in the Dort Mall. Several old Amoco and Standard signs are still at the Signs by Crannie boneyard. The major oil companies usually ask that their old, obsolete signs be destroyed. That makes the surviving vintage gas station signs very valuable. Other old gas station signs I found were for Marathon and Shell.

Bank consolidations leading to castoff signs in the boneyard are represented by a Bank One sign (replaced by Chase in 2006) and an Old Kent Bank sign (replaced by Fifth Third Bank in 2001). I only found one example of each sign, as the other signs had already been scrapped in the case of Bank One (these were mostly metal) or recycled into new signs like the Old Kent backlit box signs.

Most examples of castoff signs in the boneyard are results of updates, renovations and new logo designs. In 2004, Citizens Bank commissioned Signs by Crannie to roll out Citizens Bank's updated weather ball corporate logo in the area. As Citizens' old signs were of the backlit box variety, which could easily be reused as different signs, it was difficult to find Citizens Bank signs of the old design, but I found a horizontal box that had been mounted on a bank's façade, as well as a few directional signs. Most of the other Citizens signs are of the current variety, waiting to be installed at a new branch. Another new-look sign victim was the old Save-A-Lot box sign. Save-A-Lot is a national chain of no-frills discount supermarkets that are franchises. Kessel Enterprises (yes, big Al Kessel's company, whose Kessel supermarket chain was sold to Kroger) is the local Save-A-Lot franchisee. Shell also changed its signs, so one old design was found in the boneyard. Prime Outlets of Birch Run changed logos, so it changed signs, too. An old-design Subway restaurant sign is there, as is a Wendy's sign. An old-design K-Mart garden shop sign is there, too. Saginaw-based Team One Credit Union had an old sign. Old Troy Cleaners and Toyota signs were here, too. Oak Express, Sofa Mart and Bedroom Expressions are part of Furniture Row on Linden Road, and their castoff old signs wound up here. A Linden Road office complex, called 2222 Office Center, got a new name, Trillium Office Park, so the old 2222 sign ended up here as well.

As mentioned, the boneyard name is a misnomer; it is also a storage yard. It does not just contain signs being stored but also other items, including a converted former city bus noted in the tour. Stored signs waiting to be installed included H&R Block, BP, K-Mart, Arby's, Subway, Krispy Kreme and Buffalo Wild Wings.

There were also several out-of-town castoff signs that neither Harry nor myself recognized, as well as loose, randomly stored neon channel sign letters. Two signs do not fall into the above categories. A delivered Bennigan's sign turned out to be a wrong order, so the orphaned sign is also in the boneyard. Not in the boneyard, but in the loading area in 2006, was the old Circus Time Pizza Jell E. Bean clown sign, waiting for the permits so that it could be reinstalled at its original location in the Dort Mall, where it now stands in the mall's parking lot. Two Signs by Crannie staffers were happy that the clown sign was installed—they can't stand clowns.

Both Harry and I enjoyed the experience.

Thanks to Dan Crannie and the Signs by Crannie staff for their cooperation and assistance with this piece.

Update: Signs by Crannie's business has grown so big that it moved to a larger location in 2015 on Market Place off Bristol Road near Bishop Airport. The business sold off the old signs in the old boneyard on Commerce Drive in Flushing in 2016.

AutoWorld

It Seemed to Be a Good Idea on Paper

On February 23, 1997, the former IMA Auditorium, the last standing building of the failed AutoWorld theme park, was imploded. The implosion was, like AutoWorld, a disappointment to the general public.

Actually, the explosive charges did their job, making it much easier for the demolition crew to clear what was left of the old IMA, a well-built structure with reinforced concrete stands holding gigantic trusses that kept their shape after the building was imploded.

The Industrial Mutual Association built the IMA Auditorium in 1929 for $1.2 million on the former site of the Randall Lumber and Coal Company, previously the site of the Crapo Sawmill. Seating more then six thousand people, it was the premier venue for concerts, stage shows, dances, lectures, sporting events, exhibitions and the Shrine Circus for decades. The IMA Auditorium never made a profit in the entire fifty years it was in operation. Changes in the automotive industry brought about by the late 1970s energy crisis brought changes to the IMA. But more significant was the loss of the IMA's vending machine and food service contract with Buick, a contract it had had since 1917 but which ended on April 1, 1979. So the IMA could no longer afford to operate large arenas. The IMA Auditorium officially closed on June 18, 1979. Its final major event was a June 1 concert by Peter Frampton. The last event before closing was a benefit country music concert on June 17, with proceeds going to the Fraternal Order of Police. The co-

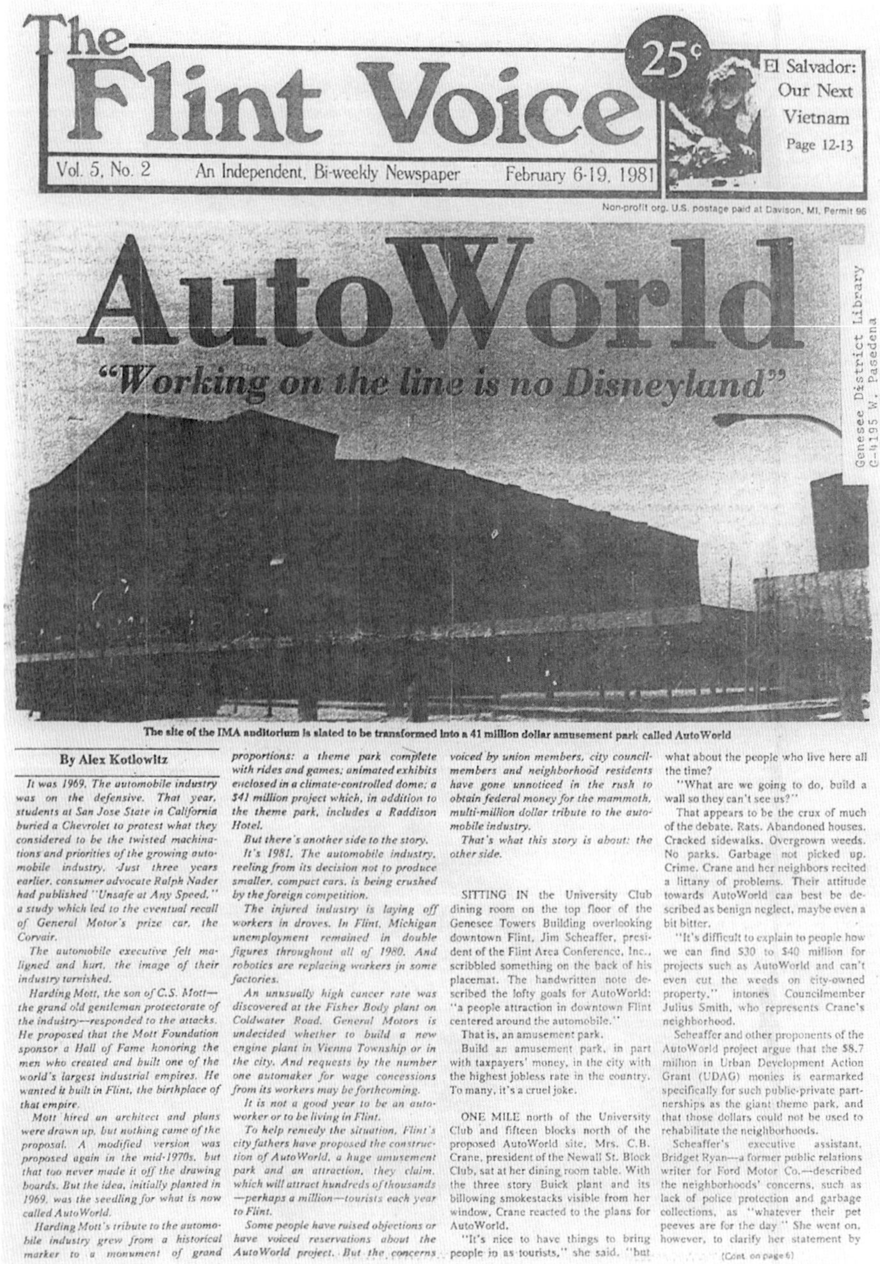

The Flint Voice

25¢

El Salvador: Our Next Vietnam

Page 12-13

Vol. 5, No. 2 An Independent, Bi-weekly Newspaper February 6-19, 1981

Non-profit org. U.S. postage paid at Davison, MI, Permit 96

Genesee District Library
G-4195 W. Pasedena
Flint, MI

AutoWorld

"Working on the line is no Disneyland"

The site of the IMA auditorium is slated to be transformed into a 41 million dollar amusement park called AutoWorld

By Alex Kotlowitz

It was 1969. The automobile industry was on the defensive. That year, students at San Jose State in California buried a Chevrolet to protest what they considered to be the twisted machinations and priorities of the growing automobile industry. Just three years earlier, consumer advocate Ralph Nader had published "Unsafe at Any Speed," a study which led to the eventual recall of General Motor's prize car, the Corvair.

The automobile executive felt maligned and hurt, the image of their industry tarnished.

Harding Mott, the son of C.S. Mott—the grand old gentleman protectorate of the industry—responded to the attacks. He proposed that the Mott Foundation sponsor a Hall of Fame honoring the men who created and built one of the world's largest industrial empires. He wanted it built in Flint, the birthplace of that empire.

Mott hired an architect and plans were drawn up, but nothing came of the proposal. A modified version was proposed again in the mid-1970s, but that too never made it off the drawing boards. But the idea, initially planted in 1969, was the seedling for what is now called AutoWorld.

Harding Mott's tribute to the automobile industry grew from a historical marker to a monument of grand proportions: a theme park complete with rides and games; animated exhibits enclosed in a climate-controlled dome; a $41 million project which, in addition to the theme park, includes a Raddison Hotel.

But there's another side to the story.

It's 1981. The automobile industry, reeling from its decision not to produce smaller, compact cars, is being crushed by the foreign competition.

The injured industry is laying off workers in droves. In Flint, Michigan unemployment remained in double figures throughout all of 1980. And robotics are replacing workers in some factories.

An unusually high cancer rate was discovered at the Fisher Body plant on Coldwater Road. General Motors is undecided whether to build a new engine plant in Vienna Township or in the city. And requests by the number one automaker for wage concessions from its workers may be forthcoming.

It is not a good year to be an autoworker or to be living in Flint.

To help remedy the situation, Flint's city fathers have proposed the construction of AutoWorld, a huge amusement park and an attraction, they claim, which will attract hundreds of thousands—perhaps a million—tourists each year to Flint.

Some people have raised objections or have voiced reservations about the AutoWorld project. But the concerns voiced by union members, city councilmembers and neighborhood residents have gone unnoticed in the rush to obtain federal money for the mammoth, multi-million dollar tribute to the automobile industry.

That's what this story is about: the other side.

SITTING IN the University Club dining room on the top floor of the Genesee Towers Building overlooking downtown Flint, Jim Scheaffer, president of the Flint Area Conference, Inc., scribbled something on the back of his placemat. The handwritten note described the lofty goals for AutoWorld: "a people attraction in downtown Flint centered around the automobile."

That is, an amusement park.

Build an amusement park, in part with taxpayers' money, in the city with the highest jobless rate in the country. To many, it's a cruel joke.

ONE MILE north of the University Club and fifteen blocks north of the proposed AutoWorld site, Mrs. C.B. Crane, president of the Newall St. Block Club, sat at her dining room table. With the three story Buick plant and its billowing smokestacks visible from her window, Crane reacted to the plans for AutoWorld.

"It's nice to have things to bring people in as tourists," she said, "but what about the people who live here all the time?

"What are we going to do, build a wall so they can't see us?"

That appears to be the crux of much of the debate. Rats. Abandoned houses. Cracked sidewalks. Overgrown weeds. No parks. Garbage not picked up. Crime. Crane and her neighbors recited a littany of problems. Their attitude towards AutoWorld can best be described as benign neglect, maybe even a bit bitter.

"It's difficult to explain to people how we can find $30 to $40 million for projects such as AutoWorld and can't even cut the weeds on city-owned property," intones Councilmember Julius Smith, who represents Crane's neighborhood.

Scheaffer and other proponents of the AutoWorld project argue that the $8.7 million in Urban Development Action Grant (UDAG) monies is earmarked specifically for such public-private partnerships as the giant theme park, and that those dollars could not be used to rehabilitate the neighborhoods.

Scheaffer's executive assistant, Bridget Ryan—a former public relations writer for Ford Motor Co.—described the neighborhoods' concerns, such as lack of police protection and garbage collections, as "whatever their pet peeves are for the day." She went on, however, to clarify her statement by

(Cont. on page 6)

The AutoWorld cover story in Michael Moore's *Flint Voice*.

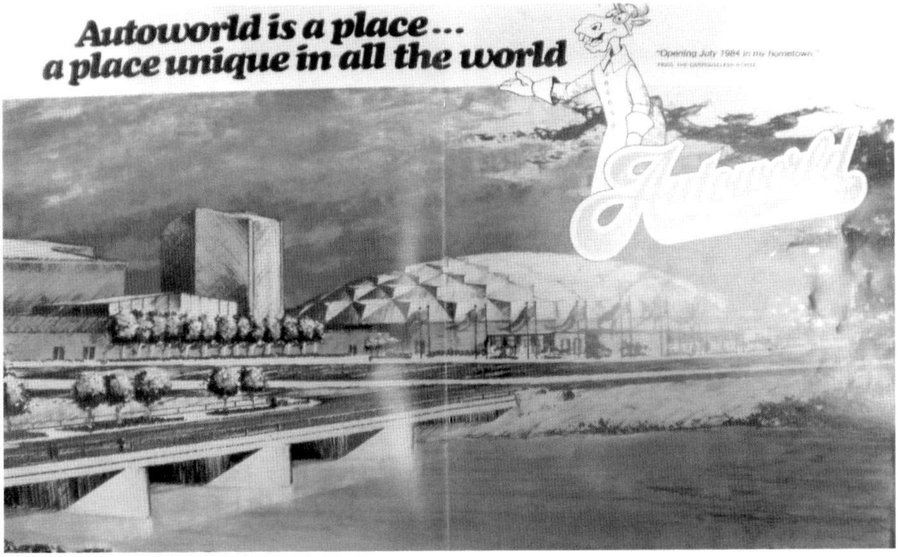

An early advertisement promoting AutoWorld during its construction, featuring ride mascot Fred the Carriageless Horse.

owned IMA Sports Arena (now the privately run Perani Arena and Events Center) was turned over to the City of Flint.

The closed auditorium was sold by the IMA to the Mott Foundation for $2.4 million and incorporated into AutoWorld, which began construction in 1982 and opened in 1984. The original concept was devised in 1969, and by 1971 an Automotive Hall of Fame had been proposed. Many changes to the proposal were made before ground was broken on AutoWorld. Nearly half of AutoWorld's construction costs were paid by the Mott Foundation.

Noted amusement park operator Six Flags operated AutoWorld, which opened on July 4, 1984, with much ballyhoo and fanfare. City leaders predicted it would double or triple the area's tourism. Unfortunately, the indoor theme park couldn't decide what it was. It had elements of a theme park, a science center, a festival marketplace and an automotive museum.

TV commercials that aired regionally made AutoWorld seem like an amusement park, but it did not have thrill rides. The rides it did have were disappointments. It did have bumper cars and a historic carousel. Needless to say, the number of paying visitors did not meet projections, and AutoWorld first closed six months after it opened. Six Flags reopened AutoWorld in 1985, adding additional attractions, including Summer Magic with outdoor entertainment and a Ferris wheel inside the dome. But after another disappointing year, Six Flags pulled out. Some believe that Six Flags' approach to AutoWorld's business model was a factor in its failure.

The IMAX Theater briefly operated on its own, with only the Wonder Wall historical exhibits open. The rest of AutoWorld was sealed off. It did open occasionally for special events, but it had closed for good by 1994. There were many proposals submitted for the AutoWorld property in 1993 to then mayor Woodrow Stanley. They included two for gambling casinos and one each for a corporate training facility, a soccer complex and a game show arena. The casino idea seemed to be the best at the time, according to Stanley, but in November 1994 Flint voters rejected a ballot proposal to convert AutoWorld into a casino by a narrow margin. This left Stanley and the Mott Foundation with the only feasible option of expanding the University of Michigan–Flint. But the university was only interested in the land, not the buildings on the land, thus sealing the fate of AutoWorld and the former IMA Auditorium in 1996.

The Mott Foundation covered the cost of demolition, which began on January 3, 1997. The AutoWorld dome and the former IMA Annex were demolished by conventional means. But the demolition contractor, Best Wrecking of Detroit, decided that the old IMA Auditorium was too sturdy a building to demolish by wrecking ball during the cold winter months. It hired a subcontractor, Engineered Demolition, to implode the building with explosives.

On the morning of the implosion, ten thousand people showed up. Most of them were at Windmill Place across Fifth Avenue from the AutoWorld site. The rest, including me, stood on the Saginaw Street Bridge. WJRT covered the implosion live beginning at 8:30 a.m. that Sunday, so before leaving to see the implosion, I set the VCR to record the event, which WJRT called "Boom for Growth." Reporter and weekend anchor Joel Feick covered the implosion from the bridge, so I saw his live reports as Feick gave them. As he covered a previous implosion in Toledo, he warned the crowd to expect a loud boom that could be felt and a thick dust cloud.

After a minor delay caused by a security breach, the explosives went off at 9:05 a.m., beginning with the southeast corner of the IMA and moving in both directions to the northwest corner. I felt the shock wave in my chest. The bricks came down, and the huge trusses dropped from front to back with the developing dust cloud. The chimney in the back billowed dust, and when the explosives went off in the back, the chimney slowly teetered before it tumbled. The crowd roared its approval. But when the dust settled, disappointment set in. The huge trusses had kept their shape, and part of the back wall was still in place. Even reporter Joel Feick thought that the implosion was not a success. When the demolition people were contacted, they said they did their job and the implosion was a success.

The IMA Auditorium did not have a basement, so when it was imploded, the debris had no place to go other than to pile up on top of itself. The wall was left standing intentionally—the demolition crew thought the debris would keep it standing anyway. The implosion made the job of clearing what was left of the IMA much easier; it took about three weeks to clear the site. The IMA bricks were sold as fundraising mementos, and some were marked for use in a memorial at IMA's Brookwood Golf Course that apparently wasn't built because the bricks were in poor condition. Material that could not be recycled was sent to the Venice Park Landfill in Shiawassee County. The only known collateral damage outside AutoWorld was a figure of Jesus that fell off a wall at St. Michael Catholic Church on the opposite corner of AutoWorld. The statue was repaired.

After the implosion, the copper box in the IMA Auditorium's cornerstone was cut open by Sloan Museum officials on March 10, 1997. The box, which had been soldered shut in 1929, was airtight and watertight, preserving its contents—to the amazement of museum staff, who put several of the artifacts on display shortly afterward.

The William S. White Building—named after the Mott Foundation official, who was, ironically, an AutoWorld booster—opened in 2002 on the former AutoWorld site.

When Hollywood Came to Flint

When the makers of the 2008 film *Semi-Pro*, starring Will Ferrell and Woody Harrelson, decided to set the film in Flint circa 1976, they showed that they care about the city by deciding to film location scenes in Flint. Those with long TV memories may recall a short-lived family show called *The Fitzpatricks*, which was also set in Flint and aired on CBS during the 1977–78 season. That show premiered on Labor Day 1977 and suffered from low ratings, so it was cancelled midseason. The final episode aired on January 3, 1978. I lost interest in the show after watching the first episode, in which the father, Mike Fitzpatrick (played by Bert Kramer), worked at a steel mill. Of course, Flint never had a steel mill. A soapbox derby scene showed mountains in the background, and you know that Flint's terrain is as flat as a pancake. Except for the film *Chameleon Street* (1989), *The Fitzpatricks* was the last fully scripted production set in Flint. All later productions set in Flint, until *Semi-Pro* came along, were documentaries, mostly by Michael Moore.

Filming for *Semi-Pro* began on Sunday, April 29, 2007, at the Top Hat Auto Wash on Hemphill Road near Fenton Road. No prep work needed to be done to the car wash before filming. While actor DeRay Davis was drying vintage cars for the film, which is set in 1976, many local residents watched from across Hemphill, at the parking lot of the South Flint Plaza. Davis played one of the members of the Flint Tropics minor-league basketball

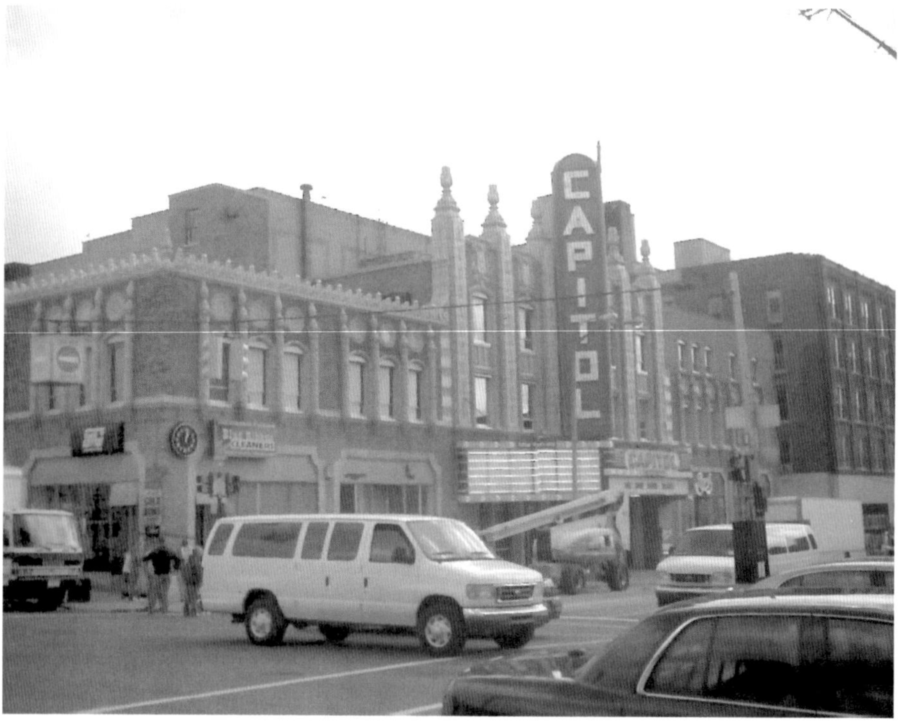

Capitol Theatre prepares for filming.

team working a second job at the car wash. Filming also took place at Atwood Stadium and the University of Michigan–Flint campus.

The real excitement came when work was done to spruce up downtown Flint. As the film's setting was wintertime Flint, piles of sand were poured along the curbs of the street, creating fake snow. Vintage signs were borrowed from Bob Perani's collection in the Dort Mall and were hung over the storefronts. But what was most exciting was that the Capitol Theatre got a makeover, which included restoring the theater's 1940s vintage marquee so that the racing lights fully function. New fluorescent backlighting was also added. Several scenes were filmed at the Capitol Theatre, including the closed-circuit Mega Bowl TV presentation, which ended up on the cutting room floor. (That was back before pay-per-view TV became widely available and events were televised via closed-circuit TV at theaters and arenas.) The messages on the marquee read, "Mega Bowl on Closed Circuit TV" on the west face, "Mother Jugs and Speed" with show times on the east face and, depending

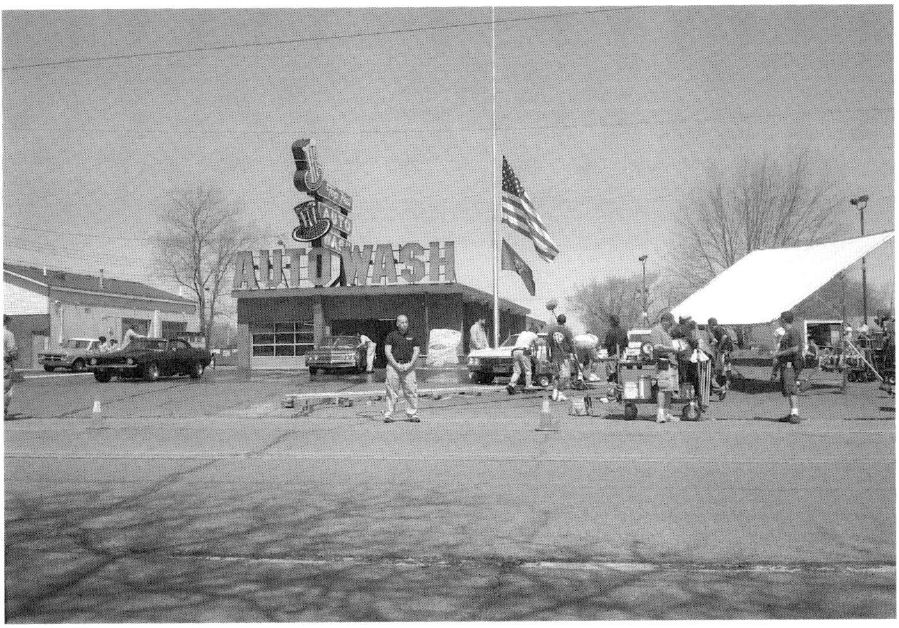

The Top Hat Auto Wash during filming. *Courtesy of Tom Wirt.*

on the scene, either *The Bad News Bears* (which co-starred Jackie Early Haley, who also co-stars in *Semi-Pro*) or *Gator* as "coming soon" on the center of the marquee. The Capitol Theatre building storefronts also got spruced up with vintage signs, again mostly from the Dort Mall collection. One sign that I thought looked out of place was the "As You Travel Ask Us" sign, which, in the 1960s, was mounted on the signs of Standard Oil (aka Amoco) stations.

Filming also took place in Detroit at the State Fairgrounds Coliseum, which portrayed the Flint Fairgrounds Coliseum, whose roofline matched that of a Los Angeles facility used for the filming of interior scenes. The big Alfred E. Neuman statue was also borrowed from the Dort Mall and used for the Detroit exterior scenes.

One vacant bar just north of the Flint River got a makeover and a neon sign mounted, identifying it as The Kremlin. I got to see the film's director, Kent Alterman, there. I wasn't quite up to staying up until two or three o'clock in the morning to catch filming at the Capitol Theatre, and I was stuck at work when daytime filming took place.

Filming wrapped up during the early morning hours of Friday, May 4. Crews remained to clean up and take the signs down. During cleanup, the fire department received an unusual call, as a pile of fake snow caught fire. The film crewmen put out that fire themselves with the water tanks they used to water down the fake snow for filming. I was hoping to take daytime pictures of The Kremlin bar, as there were plans to eventually open a real Kremlin there, but the crew took down the sign.

As the producers of *Semi-Pro* spent $20,000 to make the Capitol Theatre's marquee fully functional again, Troy Farah, whose family owns the theater building, hoped that New Line Cinema would hold the world premiere at the Capitol Theatre in February, but it was held at the Showcase (now Rave) Cinemas Flint West in Flint Township. The last time the theater was open was during Flint's sesquicentennial, the weekend of September 24 and 25, 2005. During those two days, there were free showings of classic Disney cartoons. As the one old Simplex projector still in the projection booth was not in working order, a Christie digital projector was brought in to show the cartoons. They could have done the same thing with the *Semi-Pro* world premiere. The one complication was the theater's faulty heating system. To keep the theater from freezing during the winter, two regular gas furnaces are set up in front of the theater's stage, with PVC pipes leading to two holes in an exit door to exhaust the fumes. Farah indicated that there were ways of dealing with the heating problem.

The marquee's design seems to indicate that it's of 1940s vintage. In studying the marquee's construction while Signs by Crannie was working on restoring the marquee, the ghosts of previous electrical installations seem to show that the marquee was originally lit with incandescent light bulbs. It was retrofitted with fluorescent backlighting about the time the theater was modernized in 1957. The tower sign is original to the theater and was lit with light bulbs before it was eventually refaced with neon. It seems that no one recalls when the marquee was installed, as everyone I talked to only recalled the current marquee. *Semi-Pro* was released to theaters on February 29, 2008, and was later issued in two editions on DVD, as well as Blu-Ray, on June 3, 2008.

While the Flint Fairgrounds Coliseum never existed, the marquee sign that was used at the State Fairgrounds for filming later became part of the Perani Collection at the Dort Mall, at the corner of Dort Highway and Atherton Road, and was eventually auctioned off in 2009 to make room for more collectibles.

Thanks to Troy Farah for his help with this story.

About the Author

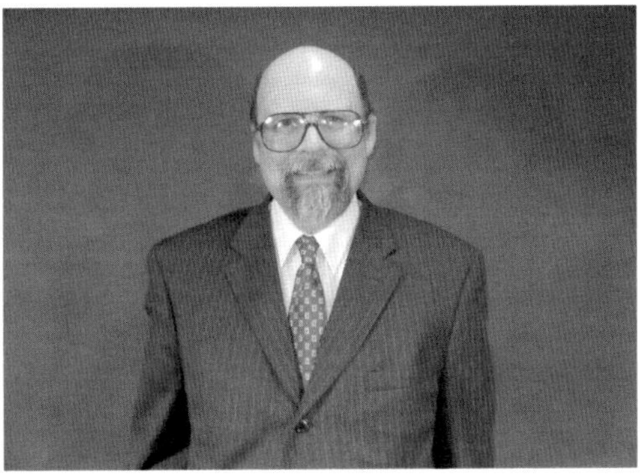

Gary Flinn is a product of the Flint Community Schools and a graduate of Mott Community College and Michigan State University who lived in the Flint area most of his life. His earliest writings were for Flint Central High School publications the *Tribal Times* and *The Arrow Head.* Besides the *Uncommon Sense,* he also contributed articles for *Your Magazine,* the *Flint Journal* and *Downtown Flint Revival* magazine. During the day, Gary Flinn helps run IO Software, a computer store in Flint. He presently lives on Flint's west side.

Visit us at
www.historypress.net

This title is also available as an e-book